MznLnx

Missing Links Exam Preps

Exam Prep for

Practical Financial Management

Lasher, 4th Edition

The MznLnx Exam Prep is your link from the texbook and lecture to your exams.
The MznLnx Exam Preps are unauthorized and comprehensive reviews of your textbooks.

MznLnx

Rico
Publications

Exam Prep for Practical Financial Management
4th Edition
Lasher

Publisher: Raymond Houge
Assistant Editor: Michael Rouger
Text and Cover Designer: Lisa Buckner
Marketing Manager: Sara Swagger
Project Manager, Editorial Production: Jerry Emerson
Art Director: Vernon Lowerui

Product Manager: Dave Mason
Editorial Assitant: Rachel Guzmanji
Pedagogy: Debra Long
Cover Image: Jim Reed/Getty Images
Text and Cover Printer: City Printing, Inc.
Compositor: Media Mix, Inc.

For more information about our products, contact us at:
Dave.Mason@RicoPublications.com

For permission to use material from this text or product, submit a request online to:
Dave.Mason@RicoPublications.com

Printed in the United States
ISBN:

Contents

TO THE STUDENT

COMPREHENSIVE

The *MznLnx* Exam Prep series is designed to help you pass your exams. Editors at MznLnx review your textbooks and then prepare these practice exams to help you master the textbook material. Unlike study guides, workbooks, and practice tests provided by the texbook publisher and textbook authors, *MznLnx* gives you ***all*** of the material in each chapter in exam form, not just samples, so you can be sure to nail your exam.

MECHANICAL

The MznLnx Exam Prep series creates exams that will help you learn the subject matter as well as test you on your understanding. Each question is designed to help you master the concept. Just working through the exams, you gain an understanding of the subject--its a simple mechanical process that produces success.

INTEGRATED STUDY GUIDE AND REVIEW

MznLnx is not just a set of exams designed to test you, its also a comprehensive review of the subject content. Each exam question is also a review of the concept, making sure that you will get the answer correct without having to go to other sources of material. You learn as you go! Its the easiest way to pass an exam.

HUMOR

Studying can be tedious and dry. MznLnx's instructional design includes moderate humor within the exam questions on occassion, to break the tedium and revitalize the brain

1. In business and accounting, _________s are everything of value that is owned by a person or company. The balance sheet of a firm records the monetary value of the _________s owned by the firm. The two major _________ classes are tangible _________s and intangible _________s.

a. EBITDA
b. Income
c. Accounts payable
d. Asset

2. In finance, a _________ is a debt security, in which the authorized issuer owes the holders a debt and, depending on the terms of the _________, is obliged to pay interest (the coupon) and/or to repay the principal at a later date, termed maturity.

Thus a _________ is a loan: the issuer is the borrower, the _________ holder is the lender, and the coupon is the interest. _________s provide the borrower with external funds to finance long-term investments, or, in the case of government _________s, to finance current expenditure.

a. Bond
b. Catastrophe bonds
c. Convertible bond
d. Puttable bond

3. In economics, a _________ is a mechanism that allows people to easily buy and sell (trade) financial securities (such as stocks and bonds), commodities (such as precious metals or agricultural goods), and other fungible items of value at low transaction costs and at prices that reflect the efficient-market hypothesis.

_________s have evolved significantly over several hundred years and are undergoing constant innovation to improve liquidity.

Both general markets (where many commodities are traded) and specialized markets (where only one commodity is traded) exist.

a. Delta hedging
b. Secondary market
c. Cost of carry
d. Financial market

4. A _________ is a professionally managed type of collective investment scheme that pools money from many investors and invests it in stocks, bonds, short-term money market instruments, and/or other securities. The _________ will have a fund manager that trades the pooled money on a regular basis. Currently, the worldwide value of all _________s totals more than $26 trillion.

Since 1940, there have been three basic types of investment companies in the United States: open-end funds, also known in the US as _________s; unit investment trusts (UITs); and closed-end funds.

a. Financial intermediary
b. Mutual fund
c. Trust company
d. Net asset value

5. A _________ is a fungible, negotiable instrument representing financial value. They are broadly categorized into debt securities (such as banknotes, bonds and debentures), and equity securities; e.g., common stocks. The company or other entity issuing the _________ is called the issuer.

a. Securities lending
b. Tracking stock
c. Security
d. Book entry

6. A _________, securities exchange or (in Europe) bourse is a corporation or mutual organization which provides 'trading' facilities for stock brokers and traders, to trade stocks and other securities. _________s also provide facilities for the issue and redemption of securities as well as other financial instruments and capital events including the payment of income and dividends. The securities traded on a _________ include: shares issued by companies, unit trusts and other pooled investment products and bonds.

a. 4-4-5 Calendar
b. 529 plan
c. 7-Eleven
d. Stock exchange

7. A _________ is a private or public market for the trading of company stock and derivatives of company stock at an agreed price; these are securities listed on a stock exchange as well as those only traded privately.

The size of the world _________ is estimated at about $36.6 trillion US at the beginning of October 2008 . The world derivatives market has been estimated at about $480 trillion face or nominal value, 12 times the size of the entire world economy.

a. Andrew Tobias
b. Anton Gelonkin
c. Adolph Coors
d. Stock market

8. A _________ is a regulated professional who buys and sells shares and other securities through market makers or Agency Only Firms on behalf of investors.

While the term _________ is still in use, it is more commonly referred to as simply 'broker', 'registered rep' or simply 'rep'--shortened versions of the official FINRA designation 'Registered Representative'. This designation is obtained by an individual passing the FINRA General Securities Representative Examination and being employed ('associated with') a registered Broker-dealer also called a brokerage firm; the firm is typically a FINRA 'member' firm.

a. Stockbroker
b. Day trader
c. Portfolio manager
d. Purchasing manager

9. _________ or financing is to provide capital (funds), which means money for a project, a person, a business or any other private or public institutions.

Those funds can be allocated for either short term or long term purposes. The health fund is a new way of _________ private healthcare centers.

a. Synthetic CDO
b. Proxy fight
c. Product life cycle
d. Funding

10. _________ is the balance of the amounts of cash being received and paid by a business during a defined period of time, sometimes tied to a specific project. Measurement of _________ can be used

- to evaluate the state or performance of a business or project.
- to determine problems with liquidity. Being profitable does not necessarily mean being liquid. A company can fail because of a shortage of cash, even while profitable.
- to generate project rate of returns. The time of _________s into and out of projects are used as inputs to financial models such as internal rate of return, and net present value.
- to examine income or growth of a business when it is believed that accrual accounting concepts do not represent economic realities. Alternately, _________ can be used to 'validate' the net income generated by accrual accounting.

_________ as a generic term may be used differently depending on context, and certain _________ definitions may be adapted by analysts and users for their own uses. Common terms include operating _________ and free _________.

_________s can be classified into:

1. Operational _________s: Cash received or expended as a result of the company's core business activities.
2. Investment _________s: Cash received or expended through capital expenditure, investments or acquisitions.
3. Financing _________s: Cash received or expended as a result of financial activities, such as interests and dividends.

All three together - the net _________ - are necessary to reconcile the beginning cash balance to the ending cash balance. Loan draw downs or equity injections, that is just shifting of capital but no expenditure as such, are not considered in the net _________.

a. Real option
b. Corporate finance
c. Shareholder value
d. Cash flow

11. In mathematics, _________ are used in the study of chance and probability. They were developed to assist in the analysis of games of chance, stochastic events, and the results of scientific experiments by capturing only the mathematical properties necessary to answer probabilistic questions. Further formalizations have firmly grounded the entity in the theoretical domains of mathematics by making use of measure theory.

a. Monte Carlo methods
b. Standard deviation
c. Variance
d. Random variables

12. _________, _________ includes the direct costs attributable to the production of the goods sold by a company. This amount includes the materials cost used in creating the goods along with the direct labor costs used to produce the good. It excludes indirect expenses such as distribution costs and sales force costs.

a. Goodwill
b. Net profit
c. Deferred financing costs
d. Cost of goods sold

13. A sole _________, or simply _________ is a type of business entity which legally has no separate existence from its owner. Hence, the limitations of liability enjoyed by a corporation and limited liability partnerships do not apply to sole proprietors. All debts of the business are debts of the owner.

a. Just-in-time
b. Product life cycle
c. Free cash flow
d. Proprietorship

14. The institution most often referenced by the word '_________' is a public or publicly traded _________, the shares of which are traded on a public stock exchange (e.g., the New York Stock Exchange or Nasdaq in the United States) where shares of stock of _________s are bought and sold by and to the general public. Most of the largest businesses in the world are publicly traded _________s. However, the majority of _________s are said to be closely held, privately held or close _________s, meaning that no ready market exists for the trading of shares.

a. Federal Home Loan Mortgage Corporation
b. Depository Trust Company
c. Corporation
d. Protect

15. _________ is the imposition of two or more taxes on the same income (in the case of income taxes), asset (in the case of capital taxes), or financial transaction (in the case of sales taxes.) It refers to two distinct situations:

- taxation of dividend income without relief or credit for taxes paid by the company paying the dividend on the income from which the dividend is paid. This arises in the so-called 'classical' system of corporate taxation, used in the United States.
- taxation by two or more countries of the same income, asset or transaction, for example income paid by an entity of one country to a resident of a different country. The double liability is often mitigated by tax treaties between countries.

It is not unusual for a business or individual who is resident in one country to make a taxable gain (earnings, profits) in another. This person may find that he is obliged by domestic laws to pay tax on that gain locally and pay again in the country in which the gain was made. Since this is inequitable, many nations make bilateral _________ agreements with each other.

a. Double taxation
b. 529 plan
c. 4-4-5 Calendar
d. 7-Eleven

16. The role of the _________ is to issue accounting standards in the United Kingdom. It is recognised for that purpose under the Companies Act 1985. It took over the task of setting accounting standards from the Accounting Standards Committee (ASC) in 1990.

a. Accounting Standards Board
b. A Random Walk Down Wall Street
c. ABN Amro
d. AAB

17. The _________ is a private, not-for-profit organization whose primary purpose is to develop generally accepted accounting principles (GAAP) within the United States in the public's interest. The Securities and Exchange Commission (SEC) designated the _________ as the organization responsible for setting accounting standards for public companies in the U.S. It was created in 1973, replacing the Accounting Principles Board and the Committee on Accounting Procedure of the American Institute of Certified Public Accountants. The _________'s mission is 'to establish and improve standards of financial accounting and reporting for the guidance and education of the public, including issuers, auditors, and users of financial information.'

The _________ is not a governmental body.

a. PlaNet Finance
b. MRU Holdings
c. Credit karma
d. FASB

18. _________ is the field of accountancy concerned with the preparation of financial statements for decision makers, such as stockholders, suppliers, banks, employees, government agencies, owners, and other stakeholders. The fundamental need for _________ is to reduce principal-agent problem by measuring and monitoring agents' performance and reporting the results to interested users.

_________ is used to prepare accounting information for people outside the organization or not involved in the day to day running of the company.

a. 4-4-5 Calendar
b. 529 plan
c. 7-Eleven
d. Financial Accounting

19. The _________ is a private, not-for-profit organization whose primary purpose is to develop generally accepted accounting principles (GAAP) within the United States in the public's interest. The Securities and Exchange Commission (SEC) designated the _________ as the organization responsible for setting accounting standards for public companies in the U.S. It was created in 1973, replacing the Accounting Principles Board and the Committee on Accounting Procedure of the American Institute of Certified Public Accountants. The _________'s mission is 'to establish and improve standards of financial accounting and reporting for the guidance and education of the public, including issuers, auditors, and users of financial information.'

The _________ is not a governmental body.

a. World Congress of Accountants
b. Federal Deposit Insurance Corporation
c. KPMG
d. Financial Accounting Standards Board

20. _________ is a concept whereby a person's financial liability is limited to a fixed sum, most commonly the value of a person's investment in a company or partnership with _________. A shareholder in a limited company is not personally liable for any of the debts of the company, other than for the value of his investment in that company. The same is true for the members of a _________ partnership and the limited partners in a limited partnership.

a. Sarbanes-Oxley Act
b. Personal property
c. Beneficial owner
d. Limited liability

21. A _________ in the law of the vast majority of United States jurisdictions is a legal form of business company that provides limited liability to its owners. It is a hybrid business entity having certain characteristics of both a corporation and a partnership or sole proprietorship (depending on how many owners there are.) The primary characteristic an _________ shares with a corporation is limited liability, and the primary characteristic it shares with a partnership is the availability of pass-through income taxation.

a. Fund of funds
b. Pension fund
c. Limited liability company
d. Financial endowment

22. In the most general sense, a _________ is anything that is a hindrance, or puts individuals at a disadvantage.

Before we discuss the financial terms, we should note that a _________ can also have a much more important slang meaning.

This is best described in an example.

a. Liability
b. McFadden Act
c. Covenant
d. Limited liability

23. _________ is used in finance as a measure of the returns that a company is realising from its capital employed. It is commonly used as a measure for comparing the performance between businesses and for assessing whether a business generates enough returns to pay for its cost of capital.

Net Profit / Capital Employed X 100

_________ compares earnings with capital invested in the company. It is similar to Return on Assets (ROA), but takes into account sources of financing.

a. Sharpe ratio
b. Net assets
c. Debt service coverage ratio
d. Return on capital employed

24. _________ measures the rate of return on the ownership interest (shareholders' equity) of the common stock owners. _________ is viewed as one of the most important financial ratios. It measures a firm's efficiency at generating profits from every dollar of shareholders' equity (also known as net assets or assets minus liabilities.)

a. Diluted Earnings Per Share
b. Return on sales
c. Return of capital
d. Return on equity

25. _________ has many definitions and is not easily analysed. In general, it represents the capital investment necessary for a business to function. Consequently, it is not a measure of assets, but of capital investment: stock or shares and long-term liabilities.

a. PEG ratio
b. Times interest earned
c. Return on assets
d. Capital employed

26. The _________ percentage shows how profitable a company's assets are in generating revenue.

_________ can be computed as:

$$\mathrm{ROA} = \frac{\text{Net Income}}{\text{Total Assets}}$$

This number tells you 'what the company can do with what it's got', i.e. how many dollars of earnings they derive from each dollar of assets they control. It's a useful number for comparing competing companies in the same industry.

a. Return on sales
b. Return on assets
c. P/E ratio
d. Receivables turnover ratio

27. _________ is a fee paid on borrowed assets. It is the price paid for the use of borrowed money , or, money earned by deposited funds . Assets that are sometimes lent with _________ include money, shares, consumer goods through hire purchase, major assets such as aircraft, and even entire factories in finance lease arrangements.

a. Insolvency
b. A Random Walk Down Wall Street
c. AAB
d. Interest

28. A mutual shareholder or _________ is an individual or company (including a corporation) that legally owns one or more shares of stock in a joint stock company. A company's shareholders collectively own that company. Thus, the typical goal of such companies is to enhance shareholder value.

a. Stock market bubble
b. Trading curb
c. Limit order
d. Stockholder

29. In political science and economics, the _________ or agency dilemma treats the difficulties that arise under conditions of incomplete and asymmetric information when a principal hires an agent. Various mechanisms may be used to try to align the interests of the agent with those of the principal, such as piece rates/commissions, profit sharing, efficiency wages, performance measurement (including financial statements), the agent posting a bond, or fear of firing. The _________ is found in most employer/employee relationships, for example, when stockholders hire top executives of corporations.

a. 4-4-5 Calendar
b. 529 plan
c. 7-Eleven
d. Principal-agent problem

30. In United States banking, _________ is a marketing term for certain services offered primarily to larger business customers. It may be used to describe all bank accounts (such as checking accounts) provided to businesses of a certain size, but it is more often used to describe specific services such as cash concentration, zero balance accounting, and automated clearing house facilities. Sometimes, private banking customers are given _________ services.

a. Cash management
b. Profitability index
c. Global tactical asset allocation
d. Capitalization rate

31. A _________ is a party (e.g. person, organization, company, or government) that has a claim to the services of a second party. The first party, in general, has provided some property or service to the second party under the assumption (usually enforced by contract) that the second party will return an equivalent property or service. The second party is frequently called a debtor or borrower.

a. False billing
b. Creditor
c. Redemption value
d. NOPLAT

32. The phrase _________ refers to the aspect of corporate strategy, corporate finance and management dealing with the buying, selling and combining of different companies that can aid, finance, or help a growing company in a given industry grow rapidly without having to create another business entity.

An acquisition, also known as a takeover, is the buying of one company (the 'target') by another. An acquisition may be friendly or hostile.

a. 4-4-5 Calendar
b. 7-Eleven
c. 529 plan
d. Mergers and acquisitions

1. _________ are formal records of a business' financial activities.

_________ provide an overview of a business' financial condition in both short and long term. There are four basic _________:

1. **Balance sheet**: also referred to as statement of financial position or condition, reports on a company's assets, liabilities, and net equity as of a given point in time.
2. **Income statement**: also referred to as Profit and Loss statement (or a 'P'L'), reports on a company's income, expenses, and profits over a period of time.
3. **Statement of retained earnings**: explains the changes in a company's retained earnings over the reporting period.
4. **Statement of cash flows**: reports on a company's cash flow activities, particularly its operating, investing and financing activities.

a. Statement of retained earnings
b. Statement on Auditing Standards No. 70: Service Organizations
c. Notes to the Financial Statements
d. Financial statements

2. _________, in bookkeeping, refers to assets, liabilities, income, and expenses recorded on individual pages of the so called book of final entry or ledger. Changes in _________ value are made by chronologically posting debit (DR) and credit (CR) entries to its page. Examples of _________s are cash, _________s receivable, mortgages, loans, land and buildings, common stock, sales, services provided, wages, and payroll overhead.

a. Option
b. Alpha
c. Accretion
d. Account

3. _________ is one of a series of accounting transactions dealing with the billing of customers who owe money to a person, company or organization for goods and services that have been provided to the customer. In most business entities this is typically done by generating an invoice and mailing or electronically delivering it to the customer, who in turn must pay it within an established timeframe called credit or payment terms.

An example of a common payment term is Net 30, meaning payment is due in the amount of the invoice 30 days from the date of invoice.

a. Accounting methods
b. Accounts receivable
c. Income
d. Impaired asset

4. _________ is a term used in accounting, economics and finance to spread the cost of an asset over the span of several years.

In simple words we can say that _________ is the reduction in the value of an asset due to usage, passage of time, wear and tear, technological outdating or obsolescence, depletion or other such factors.

In accounting, _________ is a term used to describe any method of attributing the historical or purchase cost of an asset across its useful life, roughly corresponding to normal wear and tear.

a. Bottom line
b. Matching principle
c. Deferred financing costs
d. Depreciation

5. _________, refers to consumption opportunity gained by an entity within a specified time frame, which is generally expressed in monetary terms. However, for households and individuals, '_________ is the sum of all the wages, salaries, profits, interests payments, rents and other forms of earnings received... in a given period of time.' For firms, _________ generally refers to net-profit: what remains of revenue after expenses have been subtracted.
a. Annual report
b. Income
c. OIBDA
d. Accrual

6. In finance, a _________ is a debt security, in which the authorized issuer owes the holders a debt and, depending on the terms of the _________, is obliged to pay interest (the coupon) and/or to repay the principal at a later date, termed maturity.

Thus a _________ is a loan: the issuer is the borrower, the _________ holder is the lender, and the coupon is the interest. _________s provide the borrower with external funds to finance long-term investments, or, in the case of government _________s, to finance current expenditure.

a. Convertible bond
b. Puttable bond
c. Catastrophe bonds
d. Bond

7. In finance, _________ (or gearing) is borrowing money to supplement existing funds for investment in such a way that the potential positive or negative outcome is magnified and/or enhanced. It generally refers to using borrowed funds, or debt, so as to attempt to increase the returns to equity. Deleveraging is the action of reducing borrowings.
a. Limited partnership
b. Financial endowment
c. Pension fund
d. Leverage

8. The _________ is a measure of how revenue growth translates into growth in operating income. It is a measure of leverage, and of how risky (volatile) a company's operating income is.

There are various measures of _________, which can be interpreted analogously to financial leverage.

a. Invested capital
b. Asset turnover
c. Average accounting return
d. Operating leverage

9. In business and finance, a _________ (also referred to as equity _________) of stock means a _________ of ownership in a corporation (company.) In the plural, stocks is often used as a synonym for _________s especially in the United States, but it is less commonly used that way outside of North America.

In the United Kingdom, South Africa, and Australia, stock can also refer to completely different financial instruments such as government bonds or, less commonly, to all kinds of marketable securities.

a. Margin
b. Bucket shop
c. Procter ' Gamble
d. Share

10. In economics, business, and accounting, a _________ is the value of money that has been used up to produce something, and hence is not available for use anymore. In business, the _________ may be one of acquisition, in which case the amount of money expended to acquire it is counted as _________. In this case, money is the input that is gone in order to acquire the thing.

a. Sliding scale fees
b. Fixed costs
c. Marginal cost
d. Cost

11. _________, _________ includes the direct costs attributable to the production of the goods sold by a company. This amount includes the materials cost used in creating the goods along with the direct labor costs used to produce the good. It excludes indirect expenses such as distribution costs and sales force costs.

a. Net profit
b. Cost of goods sold
c. Goodwill
d. Deferred financing costs

12. An _________ is a financial statement for companies that indicates how Revenue is transformed into net income The purpose of the _________ is to show managers and investors whether the company made or lost money during the period being reported.

The important thing to remember about an _________ is that it represents a period of time.

a. A Random Walk Down Wall Street
b. AAB
c. ABN Amro
d. Income statement

13. _________, Gross profit margin or Gross Profit Rate can be defined as the amount of contribution to the business enterprise, after paying for direct-fixed and direct-variable unit costs, required to cover overheads (fixed commitments) and provide a buffer for unknown items. It expresses the relationship between gross profit and sales revenue.

It can be expressed in absolute terms:

Gross Profit = Revenue >– Cost of Goods Sold

or as the ratio of gross profit to sales revenue, usually in the form of a percentage:

_________ Percentage = (Revenue-Cost of Goods Sold)/Revenue

Cost of goods sold includes variable costs and fixed costs directly linked to the product, such as material and labor. It does not include indirect fixed costs like office expenses, rent, administrative costs, etc.

a. 4-4-5 Calendar
b. Profit margin
c. Net profit margin
d. Gross margin

14. _________ is a fee paid on borrowed assets. It is the price paid for the use of borrowed money , or, money earned by deposited funds . Assets that are sometimes lent with _________ include money, shares, consumer goods through hire purchase, major assets such as aircraft, and even entire factories in finance lease arrangements.

a. AAB
b. Insolvency
c. A Random Walk Down Wall Street
d. Interest

15. _________ is a measure of a company's earning power from ongoing operations, equal to earnings before the deduction of interest payments and income taxes.

To accountants, economic profit, or EP, is a single-period metric to determine the value created by a company in one period - usually a year. It is the net profit after tax less the equity charge, a risk-weighted cost of capital.

a. A Random Walk Down Wall Street
b. Economic profit
c. AAB
d. Operating profit

16. _________ is the difference between price and the costs of bringing to market whatever it is that is accounted as an enterprise (whether by harvest, extraction, manufacture, or purchase) in terms of the component costs of delivered goods and/or services and any operating or other expenses.

A key difficulty in measuring profit is in defining costs. Pure economic monetary profits can be zero or negative even in competitive equilibrium when accounted monetized costs exceed monetized price.

a. AAB
b. Accounting profit
c. Economic profit
d. A Random Walk Down Wall Street

17. An _________ can be defined as a contract which provides an income stream in return for an initial payment.

An immediate _________ is an _________ for which the time between the contract date and the date of the first payment is not longer than the time interval between payments. A common use for an immediate _________ is to provide a pension to a retired person or persons.

a. Annuity
b. AT'T Inc.
c. Intrinsic value
d. Amortization

18. _________ is that which is owed; usually referencing assets owed, but the term can cover other obligations. In the case of assets, _________ is a means of using future purchasing power in the present before a summation has been earned. Some companies and corporations use _________ as a part of their overall corporate finance strategy.

a. Credit cycle
b. Cross-collateralization
c. Partial Payment
d. Debt

19. _________ is the money retained by the firm before deducting the money to be paid for taxes. _________ includes the money paid for interest. Thus, it can be calculated by subtracting the interest from E.B.I.T (Earnings Before Interest and Taxes)

E.B.T = E.B.I.T - Interest

a. A Random Walk Down Wall Street
b. ABN Amro
c. Earnings before Taxes
d. AAB

20. In financial and business accounting, _________ is a measure of a firm's profitability that excludes interest and income tax expenses.

EBIT = Operating Revenue - Operating Expenses (OPEX) + Non-operating Income

Operating Income = Operating Revenue - Operating Expenses

Operating income is the difference between operating revenues and operating expenses, but it is also sometimes used as a synonym for EBIT and operating profit. This is true if the firm has no non-operating income.

a. AAB
b. A Random Walk Down Wall Street
c. ABN Amro
d. Earnings before interest and taxes

21. The _________, effective annual interest rate, Annual Equivalent Rate (AER) or simply effective rate is the interest rate on a loan or financial product restated from the nominal interest rate as an interest rate with annual compound interest. It is used to compare the annual interest between loans with different compounding terms (daily, monthly, annually, or other.)

The _________ differs in two important respects from the annual percentage rate (APR):

1. the _________ generally does not incorporate one-time charges such as front-end fees;
2. the _________ is (generally) not defined by legal or regulatory authorities (as APR is in many jurisdictions.)

By contrast, the 'effective APR' is used as a legal term, where front-fees and other costs can be included, as defined by local law.

Annual Percentage Yield or effective annual yield is the analogous concept used for savings or investment products, such as a certificate of deposit.

a. Effective interest rate
b. A Random Walk Down Wall Street
c. ABN Amro
d. AAB

22. _________ or financing is to provide capital (funds), which means money for a project, a person, a business or any other private or public institutions.

Those funds can be allocated for either short term or long term purposes. The health fund is a new way of _________ private healthcare centers.

a. Synthetic CDO
b. Proxy fight
c. Product life cycle
d. Funding

23. In finance, a _________ is collateral that the holder of a position in securities, options, or futures contracts has to deposit to cover the credit risk of his counterparty (most often his broker.) This risk can arise if the holder has done any of the following:

- borrowed cash from the counterparty to buy securities or options,
- sold securities or options short, or
- entered into a futures contract.

The collateral can be in the form of cash or securities, and it is deposited in a _________ account. On U.S. futures exchanges, '_________' was formally called performance bond.

_________ buying is buying securities with cash borrowed from a broker, using other securities as collateral.

a. Credit
b. Procter ' Gamble
c. Share
d. Margin

24. In financial accounting, a _________ or statement of financial position is a summary of a person's or organization's balances. Assets, liabilities and ownership equity are listed as of a specific date, such as the end of its financial year. A _________ is often described as a snapshot of a company's financial condition.

a. Statement on Auditing Standards No. 70: Service Organizations
b. Financial statements
c. Statement of retained earnings
d. Balance sheet

25. In the most general sense, a _________ is anything that is a hindrance, or puts individuals at a disadvantage.

Before we discuss the financial terms, we should note that a _________ can also have a much more important slang meaning.

This is best described in an example.

a. Limited liability
b. Liability
c. Covenant
d. McFadden Act

26. _________ is equal to the income that a firm has after subtracting costs and expenses from the total revenue. _________ can be distributed among holders of common stock as a dividend or held by the firm as retained earnings. _________ is an accounting term; in some countries (such as the UK) profit is the usual term.

a. Write-off
b. Furniture, Fixtures and Equipment
c. Historical cost
d. Net income

27. In accounting, _________ refers to the portion of net income which is retained by the corporation rather than distributed to its owners as dividends. Similarly, if the corporation makes a loss, then that loss is retained and called variously retained losses, accumulated losses or accumulated deficit. _________ and losses are cumulative from year to year with losses offsetting earnings.

a. Generally Accepted Accounting Principles
b. Historical cost
c. Matching principle
d. Retained earnings

28. In business and accounting, _________s are everything of value that is owned by a person or company. The balance sheet of a firm records the monetary value of the _________s owned by the firm. The two major _________ classes are tangible _________s and intangible _________s.

a. Accounts payable
b. Asset
c. Income
d. EBITDA

29. _________ is a measure of the ability of a debtor to pay their debts as and when they fall due. It is usually expressed as a ratio or a percentage of current liabilities.

For a corporation with a published balance sheet there are various ratios used to calculate a measure of liquidity.

a. Operating leverage
b. Accounting liquidity
c. Operating profit margin
d. Invested capital

30. _________ are securities that can be easily converted into cash. Such securities will generally have highly liquid markets allowing the security to be sold at a reasonable price very quickly.This is a usual feature in real estate .

a. Book entry
b. Tracking stock
c. Securities lending
d. Marketable

31. A _________ is a fungible, negotiable instrument representing financial value. They are broadly categorized into debt securities (such as banknotes, bonds and debentures), and equity securities; e.g., common stocks. The company or other entity issuing the _________ is called the issuer.

a. Securities lending
b. Book entry
c. Tracking stock
d. Security

32. In accounting and finance, _________ is the portion of receivables that can no longer be collected, typically from accounts receivable or loans. _________ in accounting is considered an expense.

There are two methods to account for _________:

1. Direct write off method (Non - GAAP)

A receivable which is not considered collectible is charged directly to the income statement.

1. Allowance method (GAAP)

An estimate is made at the end of each fiscal year of the amount of _________. This is then accumulated in a provision which is then used to reduce specific receivable accounts as and when necessary.

a. 529 plan
b. Tax expense
c. 4-4-5 Calendar
d. Bad debt

33. The _________ is a capital budgeting metric used by firms to decide whether they should make investments. It is an indicator of the efficiency or quality of an investment, as opposed to net present value (NPV), which indicates value or magnitude.

The IRR is the annualized effective compounded return rate which can be earned on the invested capital, i.e., the yield on the investment.

a. AAB
b. ABN Amro
c. A Random Walk Down Wall Street
d. Internal rate of return

34. _________ is a list for goods and materials held available in stock by a business. It is also used for a list of the contents of a household and for a list for testamentary purposes of the possessions of someone who has died. In accounting _________ is considered an asset.

a. ABN Amro
b. A Random Walk Down Wall Street
c. AAB
d. Inventory

35. _________ or in-process inventory includes the set at large of unfinished items for products in a production process. These items are not yet completed but either just being fabricated or waiting in a queue for further processing or in a buffer storage. The term is used in production and supply chain management.

a. 529 plan
b. 4-4-5 Calendar
c. 7-Eleven
d. Work in process

36. In financial accounting, the term _________ is most commonly used to describe any part of shareholders' equity, except for basic share capital. Sometimes, the term is used instead of the term provision; such a use, however, is inconsistent with the terminology suggested by International Accounting Standards Board. For more information about provisions, see provision (accounting.)

a. Closing entries
b. FIFO and LIFO accounting
c. Reserve
d. Treasury stock

37. In accounting, a _________ is an asset on the balance sheet which is expected to be sold or otherwise used up in the near future, usually within one year, or one business cycle - whichever is longer. Typical _________s include cash, cash equivalents, accounts receivable, inventory, the portion of prepaid accounts which will be used within a year, and short-term investments.

On the balance sheet, assets will typically be classified into _________s and long-term assets.

a. Historical cost
b. Long-term liabilities
c. Write-off
d. Current asset

38. _________ plant, and equipment, is a term used in accountancy for assets and property which cannot easily be converted into cash. This can be compared with current assets such as cash or bank accounts, which are described as liquid assets. In most cases, only tangible assets are referred to as fixed.

a. Percentage of Completion
b. Petty cash
c. Remittance advice
d. Fixed asset

39. _________ refers to any one of several methods by which a company, for 'financial accounting' and/or tax purposes, depreciates a fixed asset in such a way that the amount of depreciation taken each year is higher during the earlier years of an asset's life. For financial accounting purposes, _________ is generally used when an asset is expected to be much more productive during its early years, so that depreciation expense will more accurately represent how much of an asset's usefulness is being used up each year. For tax purposes, _________ provides a way of deferring corporate income taxes by reducing taxable income in current years, in exchange for increased taxable income in future years.

a. A Random Walk Down Wall Street
b. AAB
c. Accelerated depreciation
d. ABN Amro

40. _________ is a cornerstone of accrual accounting together with revenue recognition. They both determine the point, at which expenses and revenues are recognized. According to the principle, expenses are recognized when they are (1) incurred and (2) offset against recognized revenues, which were generated from those expenses (related on the cause-and-effect basis), no matter when cash is paid out.

a. Gross sales
b. Pro forma
c. Retained earnings
d. Matching principle

41. _________ is a file or account that contains money that a person or company owes to suppliers, but hasn't paid yet (a form of debt.) When you receive an invoice you add it to the file, and then you remove it when you pay. Thus, the A/P is a form of credit that suppliers offer to their purchasers by allowing them to pay for a product or service after it has already been received.

a. Accounts payable
b. Outstanding balance
c. Accrual
d. Earnings before interest, taxes, depreciation and amortization

42. Accrual, in accounting, describes the accounting method known as _________, whereby revenues and expenses are recognized when they are accrued, i.e. accumulated (earned or incurred), regardless when the actual cash is received or paid out.

E.g. a company delivers a product to a customer who will pay for it 30 days later in the next fiscal year starting a week after the delivery. The company recognizes the proceeds as a revenue in its current income statement still for the fiscal year of the delivery, even though it will get paid in cash during the following accounting period.

a. AAB
b. A Random Walk Down Wall Street
c. Accrual basis
d. ABN Amro

43. _________ exists when one firm provides goods or services to a customer with an agreement to bill them later, or receive a shipment or service from a supplier under an agreement to pay them later. It can be viewed as an essential element of capitalization in an operating business because it can reduce the required capital investment to operate the business if it is managed properly. _________ is the largest use of capital for a majority of business to business (B2B) sellers in the United States and is a critical source of capital for a majority of all businesses.

a. 529 plan
b. Trade credit
c. Going concern
d. 4-4-5 Calendar

44. _________ is the provision of resources (such as granting a loan) by one party to another party where that second party does not reimburse the first party immediately, thereby generating a debt, and instead arranges either to repay or return those resources (or material(s) of equal value) at a later date. The first party is called a creditor, also known as a lender, while the second party is called a debtor, also known as a borrower.

Movements of financial capital are normally dependent on either _________ or equity transfers.

a. Comparable
b. Clearing house
c. Warrant
d. Credit

45. In accounting, _________ are considered liabilities of the business that are to be settled in cash within the fiscal year or the operating cycle, whichever period is longer.

For example accounts payable for goods, services or supplies that were purchased for use in the operation of the business and payable within a normal period of time would be _________.

Bonds, mortgages and loans that are payable over a term exceeding one year would be fixed liabilities.

a. Net income
b. Gross sales
c. Closing entries
d. Current liabilities

46. In a company, _________ is the sum of all financial records of salaries, wages, bonuses and deductions.

A paycheck, is traditionally a paper document issued by an employer to pay an employee for services rendered. While most commonly used in the United States, recently the physical paycheck has been increasingly replaced by electronic direct deposit to bank accounts.

a. Payroll
b. 529 plan
c. Tax expense
d. 4-4-5 Calendar

47. In economic models, the _________ time frame assumes no fixed factors of production. Firms can enter or leave the marketplace, and the cost (and availability) of land, labor, raw materials, and capital goods can be assumed to vary. In contrast, in the short-run time frame, certain factors are assumed to be fixed, because there is not sufficient time for them to change.

a. 529 plan
b. Long-run
c. Short-run
d. 4-4-5 Calendar

48. _________ is a financial metric which represents operating liquidity available to a business. Along with fixed assets such as plant and equipment, _________ is considered a part of operating capital. It is calculated as current assets minus current liabilities.

a. Working capital management
b. 529 plan
c. 4-4-5 Calendar
d. Working capital

49. _________ in its classic form is defined as a company from one country making a physical investment into building a factory in another country. It is the establishment of an enterprise by a foreigner. Its definition can be extended to include investments made to acquire lasting interest in enterprises operating outside of the economy of the investor.

a. Dow Jones ' Company
b. Public company
c. MicroPlace
d. Foreign direct investment

50. _________ is typically a higher ranking stock than voting shares, and its terms are negotiated between the corporation and the investor.

_________ usually carry no voting rights, but may carry superior priority over common stock in the payment of dividends and upon liquidation. _________ may carry a dividend that is paid out prior to any dividends to common stock holders.

a. Follow-on offering
b. Preferred stock
c. Second lien loan
d. Trade-off theory

51. An _________ is a tax levied on the financial income of people, corporations, or other legal entities. Various _________ systems exist, with varying degrees of tax incidence. Income taxation can be progressive, proportional, or regressive.

a. AAB
b. A Random Walk Down Wall Street
c. Income tax
d. ABN Amro

52. A _________ is generally conceived as a direct tax on all household wealth holdings actually accumulated as purchasing power stock (rather than flow), including owner-occupied housing; cash, bank deposits, money funds, and savings in insurance and pension plans; investment in real estate and unincorporated businesses; and corporate stock, financial securities, and personal trusts. One's wealth is the present value of income flow obtained in the future by him or her, identical to impose tax on both wealth and income obtained in the future. _________ and income one are not different from each other regarding this principle of wealth taxation.

a. 4-4-5 Calendar
b. 529 plan
c. Wealth tax
d. 7-Eleven

53. _________ are the divisions at which tax rates change in a progressive tax system (or an explicitly regressive tax system, although this is much rarer.) Essentially, they are the cutoff values for taxable income -- income past a certain point will be taxed at a higher rate.

Imagine that there are three _________: 10%, 20%, and 30%.

a. Payroll tax
b. Capital gains tax
c. Tax holiday
d. Tax brackets

54. A _________ is a profit that results from investments into a capital asset, such as stocks, bonds or real estate, which exceeds the purchase price. It is the difference between a higher selling price and a lower purchase price, resulting in a financial gain for the seller. Conversely, a capital loss arises if the proceeds from the sale of a capital asset are less than the purchase price.

a. Payroll tax
b. Tax brackets
c. Capital gains tax
d. Capital gain

55. _________ is the standard framework of guidelines for financial accounting used in the United States of America. It includes the standards, conventions, and rules accountants follow in recording and summarizing transactions, and in the preparation of financial statements. _________ are now issued by the Financial Accounting Standards Board (FASB).

a. Depreciation
b. Revenue
c. Net income
d. Generally Accepted Accounting Principles

56. Under the United States Internal Revenue Code, the type of income is defined by its character. _________ is usually characterized as income other than capital gain. _________ can consist of income from wages, salaries, tips, commissions, bonuses, and other types of compensation from employment, interest, dividends, or net income from a sole proprietorship, partnership or LLC.

a. AAB
b. A Random Walk Down Wall Street
c. ABN Amro
d. Ordinary income

57. A _________ is a payment made by a corporation to its shareholder members. When a corporation earns a profit or surplus, that money can be put to two uses: it can either be re-invested in the business (called retained earnings), or it can be paid to the shareholders as a _________. Many corporations retain a portion of their earnings and pay the remainder as a _________.

a. Special dividend
b. Dividend
c. Dividend yield
d. Dividend puzzle

58. In the United States, a _________ is a bond issued by a city or other local government, or their agencies. Potential issuers of these bonds include cities, counties, redevelopment agencies, school districts, publicly owned airports and seaports, and any other governmental entity (or group of governments) below the state level. They may be general obligations of the issuer or secured by specified revenues.

a. Puttable bond
b. Municipal bond
c. Senior debt
d. Premium bond

59. _________ is the portion of income that is the subject of taxation according to the laws that determine what is income and the taxation rate for that income. Generally, _________ refers to an individual's (or corporation's) gross income, adjusted for various deductions allowable by statute. The main questions put by most individuals in any jurisdiction are 'what makes up my _________' and what tax rates should be applied such that I can work out my tax liability to the state.

a. 4-4-5 Calendar
b. 7-Eleven
c. 529 plan
d. Taxable income

60. _________ are made by investors and investment managers.

Investors commonly perform investment analysis by making use of fundamental analysis, technical analysis and gut feel.

_________ are often supported by decision tools.

a. Investment performance
b. Investing online
c. Asset allocation
d. Investment decisions

61. _________ refers to a tax levied by various jurisdictions on the profits made by companies or associations. It is a tax on the value of the corporation's profits.

The measure of taxable profits varies from country to country.

a. First-mover advantage
b. Trade finance
c. Proxy fight
d. Corporate Tax

62. _________ is the imposition of two or more taxes on the same income (in the case of income taxes), asset (in the case of capital taxes), or financial transaction (in the case of sales taxes.) It refers to two distinct situations:

- taxation of dividend income without relief or credit for taxes paid by the company paying the dividend on the income from which the dividend is paid. This arises in the so-called 'classical' system of corporate taxation, used in the United States.
- taxation by two or more countries of the same income, asset or transaction, for example income paid by an entity of one country to a resident of a different country. The double liability is often mitigated by tax treaties between countries.

It is not unusual for a business or individual who is resident in one country to make a taxable gain (earnings, profits) in another. This person may find that he is obliged by domestic laws to pay tax on that gain locally and pay again in the country in which the gain was made. Since this is inequitable, many nations make bilateral _________ agreements with each other.

a. Double taxation
b. 7-Eleven
c. 4-4-5 Calendar
d. 529 plan

63. The institution most often referenced by the word '_________' is a public or publicly traded _________, the shares of which are traded on a public stock exchange (e.g., the New York Stock Exchange or Nasdaq in the United States) where shares of stock of _________s are bought and sold by and to the general public. Most of the largest businesses in the world are publicly traded _________s. However, the majority of _________s are said to be closely held, privately held or close _________s, meaning that no ready market exists for the trading of shares.

a. Federal Home Loan Mortgage Corporation
b. Protect
c. Depository Trust Company
d. Corporation

64. The _________ of an asset is the return obtained from holding it (if positive), or the cost of holding it (if negative)

For instance, commodities are usually negative _________ assets, as they incur storage costs, but in some circumstances, commodities can be positive _________ assets as the market is willing to pay a premium for availability.

This can also refer to a trade with more than one leg, where you earn the spread between borrowing a low _________ asset and lending a high _________ one.

a. Bankruptcy remote
b. Financial assistance
c. Cramdown
d. Carry

65. In business, _________ is income that a company receives from its normal business activities, usually from the sale of goods and services to customers. Some companies also receive _________ from interest, dividends or royalties paid to them by other companies. _________ may refer to business income in general, or it may refer to the amount, in a monetary unit, received during a period of time, as in 'Last year, Company X had _________ of $32 million.'

In many countries, including the UK, _________ is referred to as turnover.

a. Revenue
b. Matching principle
c. Furniture, Fixtures and Equipment
d. Bottom line

1. The terms _________ , nominal _________, and effective _________ describe the interest rate for a whole year (annualized), rather than just a monthly fee/rate, as applied on a loan, mortgage, credit card, etc. Those terms have formal, legal definitions in some countries or legal jurisdictions, but in general:

- The nominal _________ is the simple-interest rate (for a year.)
- The effective _________ is the fee+compound interest rate (calculated across a year.)

The nominal _________ is calculated as: the rate, for a payment period, multiplied by the number of payment periods in a year. However, the exact legal definition of 'effective _________' can vary greatly in each jurisdiction, depending on the type of fees included, such as participation fees, loan origination fees, monthly service charges, or late fees. The effective _________ has been called the 'mathematically-true' interest rate for each year. The computation for the effective _________, as the fee+compound interest rate, can also vary depending on whether the up-front fees, such as origination or participation fees, are added to the entire amount, or treated as a short-term loan due in the first payment.

a. Annual percentage rate
b. AAB
c. A Random Walk Down Wall Street
d. ABN Amro

2. A _________ is a party (e.g. person, organization, company, or government) that has a claim to the services of a second party. The first party, in general, has provided some property or service to the second party under the assumption (usually enforced by contract) that the second party will return an equivalent property or service. The second party is frequently called a debtor or borrower.

a. False billing
b. Redemption value
c. Creditor
d. NOPLAT

3. A _________, securities analyst, research analyst, equity analyst, or investment analyst is a person who performs financial analysis for external or internal clients as a core part of the job.

An analyst studies companies and other entities to arrive at the estimate of their financial value. It is normally done by analyzing financial reports, aided by follow-up interviews with company representatives and industry experts.

a. Portfolio manager
b. Purchasing manager
c. Financial analyst
d. Stockbroker

4. _________ is the standard framework of guidelines for financial accounting used in the United States of America. It includes the standards, conventions, and rules accountants follow in recording and summarizing transactions, and in the preparation of financial statements. _________ are now issued by the Financial Accounting Standards Board (FASB).

a. Net income
b. Revenue
c. Depreciation
d. Generally accepted accounting principles

5. A _________ is a fungible, negotiable instrument representing financial value. They are broadly categorized into debt securities (such as banknotes, bonds and debentures), and equity securities; e.g., common stocks. The company or other entity issuing the _________ is called the issuer.

a. Securities lending
b. Book entry
c. Security
d. Tracking stock

6. The U.S. _________ is an independent agency of the United States government which holds primary responsibility for enforcing the federal securities laws and regulating the securities industry, the nation's stock and options exchanges, and other electronic securities markets. The SEC was created by section 4 of the SEC of 1934 (now codified as 15 U.S.C. Â§ 78d and commonly referred to as the 1934 Act.)

a. 529 plan
b. 4-4-5 Calendar
c. 7-Eleven
d. Securities and Exchange Commission

7. _________ refers to an assessment of the viability, stability and profitability of a business, sub-business or project.

It is performed by professionals who prepare reports using ratios that make use of information taken from financial statements and other reports. These reports are usually presented to top management as one of their bases in making business decisions.

a. Value investing
b. Financial analysis
c. 529 plan
d. 4-4-5 Calendar

8. The _________ was the first United States Federal statute to limit cartels and monopolies. It falls under antitrust law.

The Act provides: 'Every contract, combination in the form of trust or otherwise, or conspiracy, in restraint of trade or commerce among the several States, or with foreign nations, is declared to be illegal'. The Act also provides: 'Every person who shall monopolize, or attempt to monopolize, or combine or conspire with any other person or persons, to monopolize any part of the trade or commerce among the several States, or with foreign nations, shall be deemed guilty of a felony [. . .]'

a. 4-4-5 Calendar
b. 529 plan
c. 7-Eleven
d. Sherman Antitrust Act

9. In financial accounting, a _________ or statement of cash flows is a financial statement that shows a company's flow of cash. The money coming into the business is called cash inflow, and money going out from the business is called cash outflow. The statement shows how changes in balance sheet and income accounts affect cash and cash equivalents, and breaks the analysis down to operating, investing, and financing activities.

a. 7-Eleven
b. Cash flow statement
c. 4-4-5 Calendar
d. 529 plan

10. _________ is the balance of the amounts of cash being received and paid by a business during a defined period of time, sometimes tied to a specific project. Measurement of _________ can be used

- to evaluate the state or performance of a business or project.
- to determine problems with liquidity. Being profitable does not necessarily mean being liquid. A company can fail because of a shortage of cash, even while profitable.
- to generate project rate of returns. The time of _________s into and out of projects are used as inputs to financial models such as internal rate of return, and net present value.
- to examine income or growth of a business when it is believed that accrual accounting concepts do not represent economic realities. Alternately, _________ can be used to 'validate' the net income generated by accrual accounting.

_________ as a generic term may be used differently depending on context, and certain _________ definitions may be adapted by analysts and users for their own uses. Common terms include operating _________ and free _________.

_________s can be classified into:

1. Operational _________s: Cash received or expended as a result of the company's core business activities.
2. Investment _________s: Cash received or expended through capital expenditure, investments or acquisitions.
3. Financing _________s: Cash received or expended as a result of financial activities, such as interests and dividends.

All three together - the net _________ - are necessary to reconcile the beginning cash balance to the ending cash balance. Loan draw downs or equity injections, that is just shifting of capital but no expenditure as such, are not considered in the net _________.

a. Real option
b. Corporate finance
c. Shareholder value
d. Cash flow

11. In mathematics, _________ are used in the study of chance and probability. They were developed to assist in the analysis of games of chance, stochastic events, and the results of scientific experiments by capturing only the mathematical properties necessary to answer probabilistic questions. Further formalizations have firmly grounded the entity in the theoretical domains of mathematics by making use of measure theory.

a. Standard deviation
b. Random variables
c. Monte Carlo methods
d. Variance

12. The _________ measures how long an investment with suppliers deprives a firm of cash -- it is (in the generic case of a retailer) the time between disbursement for inventory and collection on its sale. Thus, the _________ measures how risky it would be to increase this investment with suppliers in the course of expanding customer sales. However, shortening the _________ creates its own risks: while a firm could even achieve a negative _________ by collecting from customers before paying suppliers, a policy of strict collections and lax payments is not always sustainable.

a. Price/cash flow ratio
b. Return on capital employed
c. Return on sales
d. Cash conversion cycle

13. In business and accounting, _________s are everything of value that is owned by a person or company. The balance sheet of a firm records the monetary value of the _________s owned by the firm. The two major _________ classes are tangible _________s and intangible _________s.

a. EBITDA
b. Asset
c. Income
d. Accounts payable

14. _________ or financing is to provide capital (funds), which means money for a project, a person, a business or any other private or public institutions.

Those funds can be allocated for either short term or long term purposes. The health fund is a new way of _________ private healthcare centers.

a. Funding
b. Product life cycle
c. Proxy fight
d. Synthetic CDO

15. _________ plant, and equipment, is a term used in accountancy for assets and property which cannot easily be converted into cash. This can be compared with current assets such as cash or bank accounts, which are described as liquid assets. In most cases, only tangible assets are referred to as fixed.

a. Fixed asset
b. Remittance advice
c. Percentage of Completion
d. Petty cash

16. _________, in bookkeeping, refers to assets, liabilities, income, and expenses recorded on individual pages of the so called book of final entry or ledger. Changes in _________ value are made by chronologically posting debit (DR) and credit (CR) entries to its page. Examples of _________s are cash, _________s receivable, mortgages, loans, land and buildings, common stock, sales, services provided, wages, and payroll overhead.

a. Accretion
b. Option
c. Account
d. Alpha

17. In corporate finance, _________ is a cash flow available for distribution among all the security holders of a company. They include equity holders, debt holders, preferred stock holders, convertible security holders, and so on.

Note that the first three lines above are calculated for you on the standard Statement of Cash Flows.

a. Funding
b. Forfaiting
c. Free cash flow
d. Safety stock

18. The _________ is a financial ratio that measures whether or not a firm has enough resources to pay its debts over the next 12 months. It compares a firm's current assets to its current liabilities. It is expressed as follows:

$$\text{Current ratio} = \frac{\text{Current Assets}}{\text{Current Liabilities}}$$

For example, if WXY Company's current assets are $50,000,000 and its current liabilities are $40,000,000, then its _________ would be $50,000,000 divided by $40,000,000, which equals 1.25.

a. PEG ratio
b. Debt service coverage ratio
c. Current ratio
d. Sustainable growth rate

19. _________ is a measure of the ability of a debtor to pay their debts as and when they fall due. It is usually expressed as a ratio or a percentage of current liabilities.

For a corporation with a published balance sheet there are various ratios used to calculate a measure of liquidity.

a. Operating profit margin
b. Operating leverage
c. Accounting liquidity
d. Invested capital

20. In business, _________ is income that a company receives from its normal business activities, usually from the sale of goods and services to customers. Some companies also receive _________ from interest, dividends or royalties paid to them by other companies. _________ may refer to business income in general, or it may refer to the amount, in a monetary unit, received during a period of time, as in 'Last year, Company X had _________ of $32 million.'

In many countries, including the UK, _________ is referred to as turnover.

a. Furniture, Fixtures and Equipment
b. Matching principle
c. Bottom line
d. Revenue

21. The term _________ is often used to refer to the investment management of collective investments, (not necessarily) whilst the more generic fund management may refer to all forms of institutional investment as well as investment management for private investors. Investment managers who specialize in advisory or discretionary management on behalf of (normally wealthy) private investors may often refer to their services as wealth management or portfolio management often within the context of so-called 'private banking'.

The provision of 'investment management services' includes elements of financial analysis, asset selection, stock selection, plan implementation and ongoing monitoring of investments.

a. Asset management
b. A Random Walk Down Wall Street
c. ABN Amro
d. AAB

22. _________ is that which is owed; usually referencing assets owed, but the term can cover other obligations. In the case of assets, _________ is a means of using future purchasing power in the present before a summation has been earned. Some companies and corporations use _________ as a part of their overall corporate finance strategy.

a. Cross-collateralization
b. Partial Payment
c. Credit cycle
d. Debt

23. _________ is the price at which an asset would trade in a competitive Walrasian auction setting. _________ is often used interchangeably with open _________, fair value or fair _________, although these terms have distinct definitions in different standards, and may differ in some circumstances.

International Valuation Standards defines _________ as 'the estimated amount for which a property should exchange on the date of valuation between a willing buyer and a willing seller in an arm'e;s-length transaction after proper marketing wherein the parties had each acted knowledgeably, prudently, and without compulsion.'

_________ is a concept distinct from market price, which is 'e;the price at which one can transact'e;, while _________ is 'e;the true underlying value'e; according to theoretical standards.

a. T-Model
b. Debt restructuring
c. Wrap account
d. Market value

24. The _________ of a stock is a measure of the price paid for a share relative to the annual income or profit earned by the firm per share. It is a financial ratio used for valuation: a higher _________ means that investors are paying more for each unit of income, so the stock is more expensive compared to one with lower _________.

The _________ has units of years, which can be interpreted as 'number of years of earnings to pay back purchase price'.

a. Sustainable growth rate
b. Return of capital
c. Quick ratio
d. P/E ratio

25. In finance, the Acid-test or _________ or liquid ratio measures the ability of a company to use its near cash or quick assets to immediately extinguish or retire its current liabilities. Quick assets include those current assets that presumably can be quickly converted to cash at close to their book values.

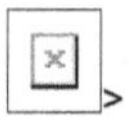
>

Generally, the acid test ratio should be 1:1 or better, however this varies widely by industry.

a. Financial ratio
b. P/E ratio
c. Quick ratio
d. Net assets

26. _________ is a list for goods and materials held available in stock by a business. It is also used for a list of the contents of a household and for a list for testamentary purposes of the possessions of someone who has died. In accounting _________ is considered an asset.

a. A Random Walk Down Wall Street
b. AAB
c. ABN Amro
d. Inventory

27. The _________ is an equation that equals the cost of goods sold divided by the average inventory. Average inventory equals beginning inventory plus ending inventory divided by 2.

The formula for _________:

$$\text{Inventory Turnover} = \frac{\text{Cost of Goods Sold}}{\text{Average Inventory}}$$

The formula for average inventory:

$$\text{Average Inventory} = \frac{\text{Beginning inventory} + \text{Ending inventory}}{2}$$

A low turnover rate may point to overstocking, obsolescence, or deficiencies in the product line or marketing effort.

a. Information ratio
b. Earnings yield
c. Inventory turnover
d. Operating leverage

28. _________ is a financial ratio that measures the efficiency of a company's use of its assets in generating sales revenue or sales income to the company.

$$Asset\ Turnover = \frac{Sales}{AverageTotalAssets}$$

- 'Sales' is the value of 'Net Sales' or 'Sales' from the company's income statement
- 'Average Total Assets' is the value of 'Total assets' from the company's balance sheet in the beginning and the end of the fiscal period divided by 2.

- Assets turnover

.

a. Asset turnover
b. Earnings yield
c. Average accounting return
d. Inventory turnover

29. _________ is one of the Accounting Liquidity ratios, a financial ratio. This ratio measures the number of times, on average, the inventory is sold during the period. Its purpose is to measure the liquidity of the inventory.

a. A Random Walk Down Wall Street
b. ABN Amro
c. AAB
d. Inventory turnover Ratio

30. _________ is a financial ratio that indicates the percentage of a company's assets are provided via debt. It is the ratio of total debt (the sum of current liabilities and long-term liabilities) and total assets (the sum of current assets, fixed assets, and other assets such as 'goodwill'.)

or alternatively:

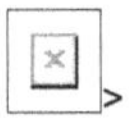

For example, a company with $2 million in total assets and $500,000 in total liabilities would have a _________ of 25%

Like all financial ratios, a company's _________ should be compared with their industry average or other competing firms.

a. Cash management
b. Capitalization rate
c. Cash concentration
d. Debt ratio

31. _________ is normally any risk associated with any form of financing.

Depending on the nature of the investment, the type of 'investment' risk will vary. High risk investments have greater potential rewards, but you may lose your money instead by taking the risk for more money.

a. Financial risk
b. Stock market index option
c. Revaluation
d. Liquidating dividend

32. _________ is a fee paid on borrowed assets. It is the price paid for the use of borrowed money , or, money earned by deposited funds . Assets that are sometimes lent with _________ include money, shares, consumer goods through hire purchase, major assets such as aircraft, and even entire factories in finance lease arrangements.

a. Insolvency
b. AAB
c. A Random Walk Down Wall Street
d. Interest

33. In accounting, _________ or *Carrying value* is the value of an asset according to its balance sheet account balance. For assets, the value is based on the original cost of the asset less any depreciation, amortization or impairment costs made against the asset. A company's _________ is its total assets minus intangible assets and liabilities.

a. Pro forma
b. Current liabilities
c. Book value
d. Retained earnings

34. In financial and business accounting, _________ is a measure of a firm's profitability that excludes interest and income tax expenses.

EBIT = Operating Revenue - Operating Expenses (OPEX) + Non-operating Income

Operating Income = Operating Revenue - Operating Expenses

Operating income is the difference between operating revenues and operating expenses, but it is also sometimes used as a synonym for EBIT and operating profit. This is true if the firm has no non-operating income.

a. A Random Walk Down Wall Street
b. ABN Amro
c. AAB
d. Earnings before interest and taxes

35. A _________ is a business that functions without the intention or threat of liquidation for the foreseeable future, usually regarded as at least within 12 months.

In accounting, '_________' refers to a company's ability to continue functioning as a business entity. It is the responsibility of the directors to assess whether the _________ assumption is appropriate when preparing the financial statements.

a. Trade credit
b. 529 plan
c. 4-4-5 Calendar
d. Going concern

36. An _________ can be defined as a contract which provides an income stream in return for an initial payment.

An immediate _________ is an _________ for which the time between the contract date and the date of the first payment is not longer than the time interval between payments. A common use for an immediate _________ is to provide a pension to a retired person or persons.

a. Intrinsic value
b. Amortization
c. AT'T Inc.
d. Annuity

37. The _________, effective annual interest rate, Annual Equivalent Rate (AER) or simply effective rate is the interest rate on a loan or financial product restated from the nominal interest rate as an interest rate with annual compound interest. It is used to compare the annual interest between loans with different compounding terms (daily, monthly, annually, or other.)

The _________ differs in two important respects from the annual percentage rate (APR):

1. the _________ generally does not incorporate one-time charges such as front-end fees;
2. the _________ is (generally) not defined by legal or regulatory authorities (as APR is in many jurisdictions.)

By contrast, the 'effective APR' is used as a legal term, where front-fees and other costs can be included, as defined by local law.

Annual Percentage Yield or effective annual yield is the analogous concept used for savings or investment products, such as a certificate of deposit.

a. Effective interest rate
b. ABN Amro
c. A Random Walk Down Wall Street
d. AAB

38. In business and finance, a _________ (also referred to as equity _________) of stock means a _________ of ownership in a corporation (company.) In the plural, stocks is often used as a synonym for _________s especially in the United States, but it is less commonly used that way outside of North America.

In the United Kingdom, South Africa, and Australia, stock can also refer to completely different financial instruments such as government bonds or, less commonly, to all kinds of marketable securities.

a. Margin
b. Share
c. Procter ' Gamble
d. Bucket shop

39. In finance, a _________ or accounting ratio is a ratio of two selected numerical values taken from an enterprise's financial statements. There are many standard ratios used to try to evaluate the overall financial condition of a corporation or other organization. They may be used by managers within a firm, by current and potential shareholders (owners) of a firm, and by a firm's creditors. Security analysts use these to compare the strengths and weaknesses in various companies.

a. Financial ratio
b. Sustainable growth rate
c. Return on capital employed
d. Price/cash flow ratio

40. In economics, business, and accounting, a _________ is the value of money that has been used up to produce something, and hence is not available for use anymore. In business, the _________ may be one of acquisition, in which case the amount of money expended to acquire it is counted as _________. In this case, money is the input that is gone in order to acquire the thing.

a. Fixed costs
b. Sliding scale fees
c. Cost
d. Marginal cost

41. The _________ is an expected return that the provider of capital plans to earn on their investment.

Capital (money) used for funding a business should earn returns for the capital providers who risk their capital. For an investment to be worthwhile, the expected return on capital must be greater than the _________.

a. Weighted average cost of capital
b. Cost of capital
c. Capital intensity
d. 4-4-5 Calendar

42. _________ is the difference between the current market value of a firm and the capital contributed by investors. If _________ is positive, the firm has added value. If it is negative, the firm has destroyed value.

a. Decision process tool
b. Market value added
c. Monetary system
d. Wrap account

43. _________ refers to the additional value of a commodity over the cost of commodities used to produce it from the previous stage of production. An example is the price of gasoline at the pump over the price of the oil in it. In national accounts used in macroeconomics, it refers to the contribution of the factors of production, i.e., land, labor, and capital goods, to raising the value of a product and corresponds to the incomes received by the owners of these factors.

a. Demand shock
b. Value added
c. Deregulation
d. Supply shock

44. _________, headquartered in Short Hills, New Jersey, USA, is a provider of credit information on businesses and corporations. Often referred to as just D'B, the company is perhaps best known for its D-U-N-S (Data Universal Numbering System) identifiers assigned to over 100 million global companies.

D'B's D-U-N-S Numbers are Business Information Reports.

a. Financial Accounting Standards Board
b. The Dun ' Bradstreet Corporation
c. FASB
d. Gold exchange-traded fund

1. In finance, the _________ is the system that allows the transfer of money between savers and borrowers.

Put another way: the _________ is a set of complex and closely interconnected financial institutions, markets, instruments, services, practices, and transactions.

a. 4-4-5 Calendar
b. Horizontal merger
c. Passive income
d. Financial system

2. _________ is a mathematical science pertaining to the collection, analysis, interpretation or explanation, and presentation of data. It also provides tools for prediction and forecasting based on data. It is applicable to a wide variety of academic disciplines, from the natural and social sciences to the humanities, government and business.

a. Covariance
b. Mean
c. Sample size
d. Statistics

3. In mathematics, _________ are used in the study of chance and probability. They were developed to assist in the analysis of games of chance, stochastic events, and the results of scientific experiments by capturing only the mathematical properties necessary to answer probabilistic questions. Further formalizations have firmly grounded the entity in the theoretical domains of mathematics by making use of measure theory.

a. Monte Carlo methods
b. Variance
c. Standard deviation
d. Random variables

4. _________ is a process by which a firm can obtain the use of a certain fixed assets for which it must pay a series of contractual, periodic, tax deductable payments. The lessee is the receiver of the services or the assets under the lease contract and the lessor is the owner of the assets. The relationship between the tenant and the landlord is called a tenancy, and can be for a fixed or an indefinite period of time (called the term of the lease).

a. Foreign Corrupt Practices Act
b. Leasing
c. Royalties
d. Quiet period

5. The _________ is the market for securities, where companies and governments can raise longterm funds. The _________ includes the stock market and the bond market. Financial regulators, such as the U.S. Securities and Exchange Commission, oversee the _________s in their designated countries to ensure that investors are protected against fraud.

a. Delta neutral
b. Forward market
c. Spot rate
d. Capital market

6. _________ are cash, evidence of an ownership interest in an entity or deliver, cash or another financial instrument.

_________ can be categorized by form depending on whether they are cash instruments or derivative instruments:

- Cash instruments are _________ whose value is determined directly by markets. They can be divided into securities, which are readily transferable, and other cash instruments such as loans and deposits, where both borrower and lender have to agree on a transfer.
- Derivative instruments are _________ which derive their value from the value and characteristics of one or more underlying assets. They can be divided into exchange-traded derivatives and over-the-counter (OTC) derivatives.

Alternatively, _________ can be categorized by 'asset class' depending on whether they are equity based (reflecting ownership of the issuing entity) or debt based (reflecting a loan the investor has made to the issuing entity.) If it is debt, it can be further categorised into short term (less than one year) or long term.

Foreign Exchange instruments and transactions are neither debt nor equity based and belong in their own category.

a. Cost of carry
b. Financial instruments
c. Secondary market
d. Financial services

7. In economics, a _________ is a mechanism that allows people to easily buy and sell (trade) financial securities (such as stocks and bonds), commodities (such as precious metals or agricultural goods), and other fungible items of value at low transaction costs and at prices that reflect the efficient-market hypothesis.

_________s have evolved significantly over several hundred years and are undergoing constant innovation to improve liquidity.

Both general markets (where many commodities are traded) and specialized markets (where only one commodity is traded) exist.

a. Cost of carry
b. Delta hedging
c. Secondary market
d. Financial market

8. _________ is a life of security. It may also refer to the final payment date of a loan or other financial instrument, at which point all remaining interest and principal is due to be paid.

1, 3, 6 months _________ band can be calculated by using 30-day per month periods.

a. Primary market
b. False billing
c. Replacement cost
d. Maturity

9. In finance, the _________ is the global financial market for short-term borrowing and lending. It provides short-term liquidity funding for the global financial system. The _________ is where short-term obligations such as Treasury bills, commercial paper and bankers' acceptances are bought and sold.

a. Cramdown
b. Debt-for-equity swap
c. Consumer debt
d. Money market

10. _________ is the amount by which a government, private company, or individual's spending exceeds income over a particular period of time, the opposite of budget surplus.

When the expenditures of a government to individuals and corporations) are greater than its tax revenues, it creates a deficit in the government budget; such a deficit is known as _________. This causes the government to borrow capital from the 'world market', increasing further debt, debt service and interest rates

a. 4-4-5 Calendar
b. 7-Eleven
c. Deficit spending
d. 529 plan

11. A _________ is an institution, firm or individual who mediates between two or more parties in a financial context. Typically the first party is a provider of a product or service and the second party is a consumer or customer.

In the U.S., a _________ is typically an institution that facilitates the channelling of funds between lenders and borrowers indirectly.

a. Net asset value
b. Savings and loan association
c. Mutual fund
d. Financial intermediary

12. The _________ is that part of the capital markets that deals with the issuance of new securities. Companies, governments or public sector institutions can obtain funding through the sale of a new stock or bond issue. This is typically done through a syndicate of securities dealers.

a. Primary market
b. Sector rotation
c. Peer group analysis
d. Volatility clustering

13. The _________ is the financial market where previously issued securities and financial instruments such as stock, bonds, options, and futures are bought and sold. The term '_________' is also used refer to the market for any used goods or assets, or an alternative use for an existing product or asset where the customer base is the second market

With primary issuances of securities or financial instruments, or the primary market, investors purchase these securities directly from issuers such as corporations issuing shares in an IPO or private placement, or directly from the federal government in the case of treasuries.

a. Performance attribution
b. Delta neutral
c. Financial market
d. Secondary market

14. _________ is that which is owed; usually referencing assets owed, but the term can cover other obligations. In the case of assets, _________ is a means of using future purchasing power in the present before a summation has been earned. Some companies and corporations use _________ as a part of their overall corporate finance strategy.

a. Partial Payment
b. Credit cycle
c. Cross-collateralization
d. Debt

15. _________ are organizations which pool large sums of money and invest those sums in companies. They include banks, insurance companies, retirement or pension funds, hedge funds and mutual funds. Their role in the economy is to act as highly specialized investors on behalf of others.

a. A Random Walk Down Wall Street
b. Institutional investors
c. AAB
d. ABN Amro

16. A _________ is a member of an exchange who is an employee of a member firm and executes orders, as agent, on the floor of the exchange for clients. The _________ receives an order via teletype machine from his firm's trading department and then proceeds to the appropriate trading post on the exchange floor. There he joins other brokers and the specialist in the security being bought or sold and executes the trade at the best competitive price available.

a. Multivariate normal distribution
b. Case-Shiller Home Price Indices
c. Business valuation standards
d. Floor broker

17. The _________ is a stock exchange based in New York City, New York. It is the largest stock exchange in the world by dollar value of its listed companies securities. As of October 2008, the combined capitalization of all domestic _________ listed companies was $10.1 trillion.

a. New York Stock Exchange
b. 7-Eleven
c. 4-4-5 Calendar
d. 529 plan

18. A _________, securities exchange or (in Europe) bourse is a corporation or mutual organization which provides 'trading' facilities for stock brokers and traders, to trade stocks and other securities. _________s also provide facilities for the issue and redemption of securities as well as other financial instruments and capital events including the payment of income and dividends. The securities traded on a _________ include: shares issued by companies, unit trusts and other pooled investment products and bonds.

a. 529 plan
b. 4-4-5 Calendar
c. 7-Eleven
d. Stock Exchange

19. A _________ is a private or public market for the trading of company stock and derivatives of company stock at an agreed price; these are securities listed on a stock exchange as well as those only traded privately.

The size of the world _________ is estimated at about $36.6 trillion US at the beginning of October 2008 . The world derivatives market has been estimated at about $480 trillion face or nominal value, 12 times the size of the entire world economy.

a. Adolph Coors
b. Andrew Tobias
c. Stock market
d. Anton Gelonkin

20. A _________ is a fungible, negotiable instrument representing financial value. They are broadly categorized into debt securities (such as banknotes, bonds and debentures), and equity securities; e.g., common stocks. The company or other entity issuing the _________ is called the issuer.

a. Security
b. Tracking stock
c. Book entry
d. Securities lending

21. The U.S. _________ is an independent agency of the United States government which holds primary responsibility for enforcing the federal securities laws and regulating the securities industry, the nation's stock and options exchanges, and other electronic securities markets. The SEC was created by section 4 of the SEC of 1934 (now codified as 15 U.S.C. Â§ 78d and commonly referred to as the 1934 Act.)

a. 529 plan
b. 4-4-5 Calendar
c. Securities and Exchange Commission
d. 7-Eleven

22. The term _________ refers to the ownership of a business company in two different ways: first, referring to ownership by non-governmental organizations; and second, referring to ownership of the company's stock by a relatively small number of holders who do not trade the stock publicly on the stock market. Less ambiguous terms for a _________ are unquoted company and unlisted company.

Though less visible than their publicly traded counterparts, private companies have a major importance in the world's economy.

a. Freshman Fund
b. Federal Deposit Insurance Corporation
c. KPMG
d. Privately held company

23. _________, is when a company issues common stock or shares to the public for the first time. They are often issued by smaller, younger companies seeking capital to expand, but can also be done by large privately-owned companies looking to become publicly traded.

In an _________ the issuer may obtain the assistance of an underwriting firm, which helps it determine what type of security to issue (common or preferred), best offering price and time to bring it to market.

a. Insolvency
b. Asian Financial Crisis
c. Interest
d. Initial public offering

24. In the United States, the Financial Industry Regulatory Authority (FINRA) is a self-regulatory organization (SRO) under the Securities Exchange Act of 1934, successor to the _________, Inc.

FINRA is responsible for regulatory oversight of all securities firms that do business with the public; professional training, testing and licensing of registered persons; arbitration and mediation; market regulation by contract for The NASDAQ Stock Market, Inc., the American Stock Exchange LLC, and the International Securities Exchange, LLC; and industry utilities, such as Trade Reporting Facilities and other over-the-counter operations.

a. 4-4-5 Calendar
b. 529 plan
c. 7-Eleven
d. National Association of Securities Dealers

25. A _________ is a payment made by a corporation to its shareholder members. When a corporation earns a profit or surplus, that money can be put to two uses: it can either be re-invested in the business (called retained earnings), or it can be paid to the shareholders as a _________. Many corporations retain a portion of their earnings and pay the remainder as a _________.

a. Dividend yield
b. Special dividend
c. Dividend puzzle
d. Dividend

26. The _________ on a company stock is the company's annual dividend payments divided by its market cap, or the dividend per share divided by the price per share. It is often expressed as a percentage.

Dividend payments on preferred shares are stipulated by the prospectus.

a. Dividend reinvestment plan
b. Dividend yield
c. Special dividend
d. Dividend imputation

27. In finance, the term _________ describes the amount in cash that returns to the owners of a security. Normally it does not include the price variations, at the difference of the total return. _________ applies to various stated rates of return on stocks (common and preferred, and convertible), fixed income instruments (bonds, notes, bills, strips, zero coupon), and some other investment type insurance products (e.g. annuities.)

a. 4-4-5 Calendar
b. Yield to maturity
c. Macaulay duration
d. Yield

28. The _________, interest yield, income yield, flat yield or running yield is a financial term used in reference to bonds and other fixed-interest securities such as gilts. It is the ratio of the annual interest payment and the bond's current price.

The _________ only therefore refers to the yield of the bond at the current moment. It does not reflect the total return over the life of the bond. In particular, it takes no account of reinvestment risk (the uncertainty about the rate at which future cashflows can be reinvested) or the fact that bonds usually mature at par value, which can be an important component of a bond's return.

a. Stochastic volatility
b. Modified Internal Rate of Return
c. Perpetuity
d. Current Yield

29. In finance, a _________ is a debt security, in which the authorized issuer owes the holders a debt and, depending on the terms of the _________, is obliged to pay interest (the coupon) and/or to repay the principal at a later date, termed maturity.

Thus a _________ is a loan: the issuer is the borrower, the _________ holder is the lender, and the coupon is the interest. _________s provide the borrower with external funds to finance long-term investments, or, in the case of government _________s, to finance current expenditure.

a. Convertible bond
b. Puttable bond
c. Catastrophe bonds
d. Bond

30. _________ is a fee paid on borrowed assets. It is the price paid for the use of borrowed money , or, money earned by deposited funds . Assets that are sometimes lent with _________ include money, shares, consumer goods through hire purchase, major assets such as aircraft, and even entire factories in finance lease arrangements.

a. A Random Walk Down Wall Street
b. AAB
c. Interest
d. Insolvency

31. _________ is an economic model based on price, utility and quantity in a market. It predicts that in a competitive market, price will function to equalize the quantity demanded by consumers, and the quantity supplied by producers, resulting in an economic equilibrium of price and quantity. Similarly, an increase in the number of workers tends to result in lower wages and vice-versa.

a. Price channel
b. Loan participation
c. Rural credit cooperatives
d. Supply and demand

32. In economics, _________ is the total amount of money available in an economy at a particular point in time. There are several ways to define 'money', but each includes currency in circulation and demand deposits.

_________ data are recorded and published.

a. 7-Eleven
b. 529 plan
c. 4-4-5 Calendar
d. Money Supply

33. An _________ is the price a borrower pays for the use of money they do not own, and the return a lender receives for deferring the use of funds, by lending it to the borrower. _________s are normally expressed as a percentage rate over the period of one year.

_________s targets are also a vital tool of monetary policy and are used to control variables like investment, inflation, and unemployment.

a. ABN Amro
b. Interest rate
c. A Random Walk Down Wall Street
d. AAB

34. In economics, _________ is a rise in the general level of prices of goods and services in an economy over a period of time. The term '_________' once referred to increases in the money supply (monetary _________); however, economic debates about the relationship between money supply and price levels have led to its primary use today in describing price _________. _________ can also be described as a decline in the real value of money--a loss of purchasing power in the medium of exchange which is also the monetary unit of account.

a. Inflation
b. A Random Walk Down Wall Street
c. AAB
d. ABN Amro

35. _________ is the process of adjusting economic indicators and the prices of goods and services from different time periods to the same price level. To adjust for inflation, an indicator is divided by the inflation index.

It is easy to show that 7% inflation, lasting 10 years, would nearly double the cost of living (1.0710=1.96.)

a. AAB
b. A Random Walk Down Wall Street
c. Inflation adjustment
d. ABN Amro

36.

In finance, the _________ can be the expected rate of return above the risk-free interest rate. When measuring risk, a common sense approach is to compare the risk-free return on T-bills and the very risky return on other investments. The difference between these two returns can be interpreted as a measure of the excess return on the average risky asset. This excess return is known as the _________.

a. Risk aversion
b. Risk adjusted return on capital
c. Risk modeling
d. Risk premium

37. _________ means regulating, adapting or settling in a variety of contexts:

In commercial law, _________ means the settlement of a loss incurred on insured goods. The calculation of the amounts of compensation to be paid by or to the several interests is a complicated matter. It involves much detail and arithmetic, and requires a full and accurate knowledge of the principles of the subject.

a. Asset recovery
b. Intelligent investor
c. Adjustment
d. Equity method

38. In finance, _________ occurs when a debtor has not met its legal obligations according to the debt contract, e.g. it has not made a scheduled payment, or has violated a loan covenant (condition) of the debt contract. _________ may occur if the debtor is either unwilling or unable to pay their debt. This can occur with all debt obligations including bonds, mortgages, loans, and promissory notes.

a. Default
b. Vendor finance
c. Credit crunch
d. Debt validation

39. _________ is the risk of loss due to a debtor's non-payment of a loan or other line of credit (either the principal or interest (coupon) or both)

Most lenders employ their own models (credit scorecards) to rank potential and existing customers according to risk, and then apply appropriate strategies. With products such as unsecured personal loans or mortgages, lenders charge a higher price for higher risk customers and vice versa. With revolving products such as credit cards and overdrafts, risk is controlled through careful setting of credit limits.

a. Liquidity risk
b. Transaction risk
c. Market risk
d. Credit risk

40. _________ is a measure of the ability of a debtor to pay their debts as and when they fall due. It is usually expressed as a ratio or a percentage of current liabilities.

For a corporation with a published balance sheet there are various ratios used to calculate a measure of liquidity.

a. Operating leverage
b. Invested capital
c. Accounting liquidity
d. Operating profit margin

41. _________ arises from situations in which a party interested in trading an asset cannot do it because nobody in the market wants to trade that asset. _________ becomes particularly important to parties who are about to hold or currently hold an asset, since it affects their ability to trade.

Manifestation of _________ is very different from a drop of price to zero.

a. Liquidity risk
b. Currency risk
c. Tracking error
d. Credit risk

42. _________ is the risk (variability in value) borne by an interest-bearing asset, such as a loan or a bond, due to variability of interest rates. In general, as rates rise, the price of a fixed rate bond will fall, and vice versa. _________ is commonly measured by the bond's duration.

a. International Fisher effect
b. Official bank rate
c. A Random Walk Down Wall Street
d. Interest rate risk

43. _________ are government bonds issued by the United States Department of the Treasury through the Bureau of the Public Debt. They are the debt financing instruments of the U.S. Federal government, and they are often referred to simply as Treasuries or Treasurys. There are four types of marketable _________: Treasury bills, Treasury notes, Treasury bonds, and Treasury Inflation Protected Securities (TIPS.)

a. 4-4-5 Calendar
b. Treasury Inflation-Protected Securities
c. Treasury Inflation Protected Securities
d. Treasury securities

44. In finance, the _________ is the relation between the interest rate (or cost of borrowing) and the time to maturity of the debt for a given borrower in a given currency. For example, the current U.S. dollar interest rates paid on U.S. Treasury securities for various maturities are closely watched by many traders, and are commonly plotted on a graph such as the one on the right which is informally called 'the _________.' More formal mathematical descriptions of this relation are often called the term structure of interest rates.

The yield of a debt instrument is the annualized percentage increase in the value of the investment.

a. 529 plan
b. 7-Eleven
c. 4-4-5 Calendar
d. Yield curve

45. John Maynard Keynes developed the _________ of Interest in the General Theory of Employment Interest and Money. The primary consideration of the _________ is the demand for money as an asset, as a means for holding wealth. Interest rates, he argues, cannot be a reward for savings as such because, if a person hoards his savings in cash, keeping it under his mattress say, he will receive no interest, although he has nevertheless, refrained from consuming all his current income.

a. Liquidity preference
b. 7-Eleven
c. 4-4-5 Calendar
d. 529 plan

1. In finance, the value of an option consists of two components, its intrinsic value and its _________. Time value is simply the difference between option value and intrinsic value. _________ is also known as theta, extrinsic value, or instrumental value.

a. Global Squeeze
b. Debt buyer
c. Conservatism
d. Time value

2. A '_________' is a 'Charge' that is paid to obtain the right to delay a payment. Essentially, the payer purchases the right to make a given payment in the future instead of in the Present. The '_________', or 'Charge' that must be paid to delay the payment, is simply the difference between what the payment amount would be if it were paid in the present and what the payment amount would be paid if it were paid in the future.

a. Risk aversion
b. Risk modeling
c. Discount
d. Value at risk

3. In finance, the _________ approach describes a method of valuing a project, company, or asset using the concepts of the time value of money. All future cash flows are estimated and discounted to give their present values. The discount rate used is generally the appropriate cost of capital and may incorporate judgments of the uncertainty (riskiness) of the future cash flows.

a. Net present value
b. Future-oriented
c. Present value of benefits
d. Discounted cash flow

4. _________ measures the nominal future sum of money that a given sum of money is 'worth' at a specified time in the future assuming a certain interest rate rate of return; it is the present value multiplied by the accumulation function.

The value does not include corrections for inflation or other factors that affect the true value of money in the future. This is used in time value of money calculations.

a. Discounted cash flow
b. Future-oriented
c. Present value of costs
d. Future value

5. _________ is the value on a given date of a future payment or series of future payments, discounted to reflect the time value of money and other factors such as investment risk. _________ calculations are widely used in business and economics to provide a means to compare cash flows at different times on a meaningful 'like to like' basis.

The most commonly applied model of the time value of money is compound interest.

a. Present value of benefits
b. Present value
c. Negative gearing
d. Net present value

6. _________ is the balance of the amounts of cash being received and paid by a business during a defined period of time, sometimes tied to a specific project. Measurement of _________ can be used

- to evaluate the state or performance of a business or project.
- to determine problems with liquidity. Being profitable does not necessarily mean being liquid. A company can fail because of a shortage of cash, even while profitable.
- to generate project rate of returns. The time of _________s into and out of projects are used as inputs to financial models such as internal rate of return, and net present value.
- to examine income or growth of a business when it is believed that accrual accounting concepts do not represent economic realities. Alternately, _________ can be used to 'validate' the net income generated by accrual accounting.

_________ as a generic term may be used differently depending on context, and certain _________ definitions may be adapted by analysts and users for their own uses. Common terms include operating _________ and free _________.

_________s can be classified into:

1. Operational _________s: Cash received or expended as a result of the company's core business activities.
2. Investment _________s: Cash received or expended through capital expenditure, investments or acquisitions.
3. Financing _________s: Cash received or expended as a result of financial activities, such as interests and dividends.

All three together - the net _________ - are necessary to reconcile the beginning cash balance to the ending cash balance. Loan draw downs or equity injections, that is just shifting of capital but no expenditure as such, are not considered in the net _________.

a. Shareholder value
b. Cash flow
c. Corporate finance
d. Real option

7. In mathematics, _________ are used in the study of chance and probability. They were developed to assist in the analysis of games of chance, stochastic events, and the results of scientific experiments by capturing only the mathematical properties necessary to answer probabilistic questions. Further formalizations have firmly grounded the entity in the theoretical domains of mathematics by making use of measure theory.

a. Variance
b. Standard deviation
c. Monte Carlo methods
d. Random variables

8. In economics, business, and accounting, a _________ is the value of money that has been used up to produce something, and hence is not available for use anymore. In business, the _________ may be one of acquisition, in which case the amount of money expended to acquire it is counted as _________. In this case, money is the input that is gone in order to acquire the thing.

a. Marginal cost
b. Sliding scale fees
c. Fixed costs
d. Cost

9. _________ or economic opportunity loss is the value of the next best alternative foregone as the result of making a decision. _________ analysis is an important part of a company's decision-making processes but is not treated as an actual cost in any financial statement. The next best thing that a person can engage in is referred to as the _________ of doing the best thing and ignoring the next best thing to be done.

a. A Random Walk Down Wall Street
b. Opportunity cost
c. ABN Amro
d. AAB

10. The _________ is a capital budgeting metric used by firms to decide whether they should make investments. It is an indicator of the efficiency or quality of an investment, as opposed to net present value (NPV), which indicates value or magnitude.

The IRR is the annualized effective compounded return rate which can be earned on the invested capital, i.e., the yield on the investment.

a. Internal rate of return
b. ABN Amro
c. A Random Walk Down Wall Street
d. AAB

11. An _________ can be defined as a contract which provides an income stream in return for an initial payment.

An immediate _________ is an _________ for which the time between the contract date and the date of the first payment is not longer than the time interval between payments. A common use for an immediate _________ is to provide a pension to a retired person or persons.

a. Amortization
b. AT'T Inc.
c. Intrinsic value
d. Annuity

12. A _________ is a fund established by a government agency or business for the purpose of reducing debt.

The _________ was first used in Great Britain in the 18th century to reduce national debt. While used by Robert Walpole in 1716 and effectively in the 1720s and early 1730s, it originated in the commercial tax syndicates of the Italian peninsula of the 14th century to retire redeemable public debt of those cities.

a. Modern portfolio theory
b. Security interest
c. Debtor
d. Sinking fund

13. _________ is the concept of adding accumulated interest back to the principal, so that interest is earned on interest from that moment on. The act of declaring interest to be principal is called compounding (i.e., interest is compounded.) A loan, for example, may have its interest compounded every month: in this case, a loan with $100 principal and 1% interest per month would have a balance of $101 at the end of the first month.

a. 4-4-5 Calendar
b. Risk management
c. Compound interest
d. Penny stock

14. _________ is a fee paid on borrowed assets. It is the price paid for the use of borrowed money , or, money earned by deposited funds . Assets that are sometimes lent with _________ include money, shares, consumer goods through hire purchase, major assets such as aircraft, and even entire factories in finance lease arrangements.

a. Insolvency
b. AAB
c. A Random Walk Down Wall Street
d. Interest

15. The terms _________ , nominal _________, and effective _________ describe the interest rate for a whole year (annualized), rather than just a monthly fee/rate, as applied on a loan, mortgage, credit card, etc. Those terms have formal, legal definitions in some countries or legal jurisdictions, but in general:

- The nominal _________ is the simple-interest rate (for a year.)
- The effective _________ is the fee+compound interest rate (calculated across a year.)

The nominal _________ is calculated as: the rate, for a payment period, multiplied by the number of payment periods in a year. However, the exact legal definition of 'effective _________' can vary greatly in each jurisdiction, depending on the type of fees included, such as participation fees, loan origination fees, monthly service charges, or late fees. The effective _________ has been called the 'mathematically-true' interest rate for each year. The computation for the effective _________, as the fee+compound interest rate, can also vary depending on whether the up-front fees, such as origination or participation fees, are added to the entire amount, or treated as a short-term loan due in the first payment.

a. AAB
b. A Random Walk Down Wall Street
c. Annual percentage rate
d. ABN Amro

16. The _________, effective annual interest rate, Annual Equivalent Rate (AER) or simply effective rate is the interest rate on a loan or financial product restated from the nominal interest rate as an interest rate with annual compound interest. It is used to compare the annual interest between loans with different compounding terms (daily, monthly, annually, or other.)

The _________ differs in two important respects from the annual percentage rate (APR):

1. the _________ generally does not incorporate one-time charges such as front-end fees;
2. the _________ is (generally) not defined by legal or regulatory authorities (as APR is in many jurisdictions.)

By contrast, the 'effective APR' is used as a legal term, where front-fees and other costs can be included, as defined by local law.

Annual Percentage Yield or effective annual yield is the analogous concept used for savings or investment products, such as a certificate of deposit.

a. ABN Amro
b. AAB
c. A Random Walk Down Wall Street
d. Effective interest rate

17. In finance and economics _________ refers to the rate of interest before adjustment for inflation (in contrast with the real interest rate); or, for interest balls stated' without adjustment for the full effect of compounding (also referred to as the nominal annual rate.) An interest rate is called nominal if the frequency of compounding (e.g. a month) is not identical to the basic time unit (normally a year.)

The real interest rate includes compensation for the lender's lost value due to inflation, whereas the _________ excludes inflation.

a. Cash accumulation equation
b. SIBOR
c. Shanghai Interbank Offered Rate
d. Nominal interest rate

18. An _________ is the price a borrower pays for the use of money they do not own, and the return a lender receives for deferring the use of funds, by lending it to the borrower. _________s are normally expressed as a percentage rate over the period of one year.

_________s targets are also a vital tool of monetary policy and are used to control variables like investment, inflation, and unemployment.

a. ABN Amro
b. A Random Walk Down Wall Street
c. AAB
d. Interest rate

19. An _________ is a retirement plan account that provides some tax advantages for retirement savings in the United States.

a. Individual Retirement Arrangement
b. ABN Amro
c. AAB
d. A Random Walk Down Wall Street

20. _________ is the process of decreasing an amount over a period of time. The word comes from Middle English amortisen to kill, alienate in mortmain, from Anglo-French amorteser, alteration of amortir, from Vulgar Latin admortire to kill, from Latin ad- + mort-, mors death. Particular instances of the term include:

- _________ (business), the allocation of a lump sum amount to different time periods, particularly for loans and other forms of finance, including related interest or other finance charges.
    - _________ schedule, a table detailing each periodic payment on a loan (typically a mortgage), as generated by an _________ calculator.
    - Negative _________, an _________ schedule where the loan amount actually increases through not paying the full interest
- Amortized analysis, analyzing the execution cost of algorithms over a sequence of operations.
- _________ of capital expenditures of certain assets under accounting rules, particularly intangible assets, in a manner analogous to depreciation.
- _________ (tax law)

_________ is also used in the context of zoning regulations and describes the time in which a property owner has to relocate when the property's use constitutes a preexisting nonconforming use under zoning regulations.

- Depreciation

.

a. Option
b. Amortization
c. AT'T Inc.
d. Intrinsic value

21. An _________ is a table detailing each periodic payment on a amortizing loan (typically a mortgage), as generated by an amortization calculator.

While a portion of every payment is applied towards both the interest and the principal balance of the loan, the exact amount applied to principal each time varies (with the remainder going to interest.) An _________ reveals the specific monetary amount put towards interest, as well as the specific put towards the Principal balance, with each payment.

a. Adjusted basis
b. Adjusting entries
c. Amortization schedule
d. Annual report

22. In finance, a _________ is a debt security, in which the authorized issuer owes the holders a debt and, depending on the terms of the _________, is obliged to pay interest (the coupon) and/or to repay the principal at a later date, termed maturity.

Thus a _________ is a loan: the issuer is the borrower, the _________ holder is the lender, and the coupon is the interest. _________s provide the borrower with external funds to finance long-term investments, or, in the case of government _________s, to finance current expenditure.

a. Puttable bond
b. Catastrophe bonds
c. Convertible bond
d. Bond

23. A _________ is an annuity in which the periodic payments begin on a fixed date and continue indefinitely. It is sometimes referred to as a perpetual annuity. Fixed coupon payments on permanently invested (irredeemable) sums of money are prime examples of these. Scholarships paid perpetually from an endowment fit the definition of _________.

a. LIBOR market model
b. Stochastic volatility
c. Current yield
d. Perpetuity

24. _________ are the earnings returned on the initial investment amount.

In the US, the Financial Accounting Standards Board (FASB) requires companies' income statements to report _________ for each of the major categories of the income statement: continuing operations, discontinued operations, extraordinary items, and net income.

The _________ formula does not include preferred dividends for categories outside of continued operations and net income.

a. Average accounting return
b. Earnings per share
c. Inventory turnover
d. Assets turnover

25. In business and finance, a _________ (also referred to as equity _________) of stock means a _________ of ownership in a corporation (company.) In the plural, stocks is often used as a synonym for _________s especially in the United States, but it is less commonly used that way outside of North America.

In the United Kingdom, South Africa, and Australia, stock can also refer to completely different financial instruments such as government bonds or, less commonly, to all kinds of marketable securities.

a. Bucket shop
b. Margin
c. Procter ' Gamble
d. Share

1. In finance, a _________ is a debt security, in which the authorized issuer owes the holders a debt and, depending on the terms of the _________, is obliged to pay interest (the coupon) and/or to repay the principal at a later date, termed maturity.

Thus a _________ is a loan: the issuer is the borrower, the _________ holder is the lender, and the coupon is the interest. _________s provide the borrower with external funds to finance long-term investments, or, in the case of government _________s, to finance current expenditure.

a. Catastrophe bonds
b. Convertible bond
c. Bond
d. Puttable bond

2. _________ is the process of determining the fair price of a bond. As with any security or capital investment, the fair value of a bond is the present value of the stream of cash flows it is expected to generate. Hence, the price or value of a bond is determined by discounting the bond's expected cash flows to the present using the appropriate discount rate.

a. Catastrophe bonds
b. Bond fund
c. Bond valuation
d. Collateralized debt obligations

3. _________ is the balance of the amounts of cash being received and paid by a business during a defined period of time, sometimes tied to a specific project. Measurement of _________ can be used

- to evaluate the state or performance of a business or project.
- to determine problems with liquidity. Being profitable does not necessarily mean being liquid. A company can fail because of a shortage of cash, even while profitable.
- to generate project rate of returns. The time of _________s into and out of projects are used as inputs to financial models such as internal rate of return, and net present value.
- to examine income or growth of a business when it is believed that accrual accounting concepts do not represent economic realities. Alternately, _________ can be used to 'validate' the net income generated by accrual accounting.

_________ as a generic term may be used differently depending on context, and certain _________ definitions may be adapted by analysts and users for their own uses. Common terms include operating _________ and free _________.

_________s can be classified into:

1. Operational _________s: Cash received or expended as a result of the company's core business activities.
2. Investment _________s: Cash received or expended through capital expenditure, investments or acquisitions.
3. Financing _________s: Cash received or expended as a result of financial activities, such as interests and dividends.

All three together - the net _________ - are necessary to reconcile the beginning cash balance to the ending cash balance. Loan draw downs or equity injections, that is just shifting of capital but no expenditure as such, are not considered in the net _________.

a. Real option b. Corporate finance
c. Shareholder value d. Cash flow

4. _________, refers to consumption opportunity gained by an entity within a specified time frame, which is generally expressed in monetary terms. However, for households and individuals, '_________ is the sum of all the wages, salaries, profits, interests payments, rents and other forms of earnings received... in a given period of time.' For firms, _________ generally refers to net-profit: what remains of revenue after expenses have been subtracted.
a. OIBDA b. Accrual
c. Annual report d. Income

5. In finance, _________ is the process of estimating the potential market value of a financial asset or liability. they can be done on assets (for example, investments in marketable securities such as stocks, options, business enterprises, or intangible assets such as patents and trademarks) or on liabilities (e.g., Bonds issued by a company.) _________s are required in many contexts including investment analysis, capital budgeting, merger and acquisition transactions, financial reporting, taxable events to determine the proper tax liability, and in litigation.
a. Procter ' Gamble b. Valuation
c. Share d. Margin

6. In mathematics, _________ are used in the study of chance and probability. They were developed to assist in the analysis of games of chance, stochastic events, and the results of scientific experiments by capturing only the mathematical properties necessary to answer probabilistic questions. Further formalizations have firmly grounded the entity in the theoretical domains of mathematics by making use of measure theory.
a. Variance b. Monte Carlo methods
c. Random variables d. Standard deviation

7. _________ is a fee paid on borrowed assets. It is the price paid for the use of borrowed money , or, money earned by deposited funds . Assets that are sometimes lent with _________ include money, shares, consumer goods through hire purchase, major assets such as aircraft, and even entire factories in finance lease arrangements.
a. Interest b. AAB
c. Insolvency d. A Random Walk Down Wall Street

8. A _________, referred to as a note payable in accounting, is a contract where one party (the maker or issuer) makes an unconditional promise in writing to pay a sum of money to the other (the payee), either at a fixed or determinable future time or on demand of the payee, under specific terms. They differ from IOUs in that they contain a specific promise to pay, rather than simply acknowledging that a debt exists.

The terms of a note typically include the principal amount, the interest rate if any, and the maturity date.

a. Financial plan b. Title loan
c. Credit repair software d. Promissory note

9. In finance, the term _________ describes the amount in cash that returns to the owners of a security. Normally it does not include the price variations, at the difference of the total return. _________ applies to various stated rates of return on stocks (common and preferred, and convertible), fixed income instruments (bonds, notes, bills, strips, zero coupon), and some other investment type insurance products (e.g. annuities.)

a. Macaulay duration
b. Yield
c. Yield to maturity
d. 4-4-5 Calendar

10. _________ is a life of security. It may also refer to the final payment date of a loan or other financial instrument, at which point all remaining interest and principal is due to be paid.

1, 3, 6 months _________ band can be calculated by using 30-day per month periods.

a. False billing
b. Replacement cost
c. Primary market
d. Maturity

11. The coupon or _________ of a bond is the amount of interest paid per year expressed as a percentage of the face value of the bond.

For example if you hold $10,000 nominal of a bond described as a 4.5% loan stock, you will receive $450 in interest each year (probably in two installments of $225 each.)

Not all bonds have coupons.

a. Puttable bond
b. Zero-coupon bond
c. Revenue bonds
d. Coupon rate

12. _________, in finance and accounting, means stated value or face value. From this comes the expressions at par (at the _________), over par (over _________) and under par (under _________.)

The term '_________' has several meanings depending on context and geography.

a. FIDC
b. Global Squeeze
c. Sinking fund
d. Par value

13. The _________ is a capital budgeting metric used by firms to decide whether they should make investments. It is an indicator of the efficiency or quality of an investment, as opposed to net present value (NPV), which indicates value or magnitude.

The IRR is the annualized effective compounded return rate which can be earned on the invested capital, i.e., the yield on the investment.

a. A Random Walk Down Wall Street
b. ABN Amro
c. AAB
d. Internal rate of return

14. An _________ is the price a borrower pays for the use of money they do not own, and the return a lender receives for deferring the use of funds, by lending it to the borrower. _________s are normally expressed as a percentage rate over the period of one year.

_________s targets are also a vital tool of monetary policy and are used to control variables like investment, inflation, and unemployment.

a. Interest rate
b. A Random Walk Down Wall Street
c. AAB
d. ABN Amro

15. The _________ or redemption yield is the yield promised to the bondholder on the assumption that the bond or other fixed-interest security such as gilts will be held to maturity, that all coupon and principal payments will be made and coupon payments are reinvested at the bond's promised yield at the same rate as invested. It is a measure of the return of the bond. This technique in theory allows investors to calculate the fair value of different financial instruments.

a. 4-4-5 Calendar
b. Yield
c. Macaulay duration
d. Yield to maturity

16. In financial accounting, _________s are precautions for which the amount or probability of occurrence are not known. Typical examples are _________s for warranty costs and _________ for taxes the term reserve is used instead of term _________; such a use, however, is inconsistent with the terminology suggested by International Accounting Standards Board.

a. Momentum Accounting and Triple-Entry Bookkeeping
b. Petty cash
c. Money measurement concept
d. Provision

17. A _________ is a bond bought at a price lower than its face value, with the face value repaid at the time of maturity. It does not make periodic interest payments, or so-called 'coupons,' hence the term zero-coupon bond. Investors earn return from the compounded interest all paid at maturity plus the difference between the discounted price of the bond and its par value.

a. Callable bond
b. Bowie bonds
c. Municipal bond
d. Zero coupon bond

18. An _________ is a contract written by a seller that conveys to the buyer the right -- but not the obligation -- to buy (in the case of a call _________) or to sell (in the case of a put _________) a particular asset, such as a piece of property such as, among others, a futures contract. In return for granting the _________, the seller collects a payment (the premium) from the buyer.

For example, buying a call _________ provides the right to buy a specified quantity of a security at a set strike price at some time on or before expiration, while buying a put _________ provides the right to sell.

a. Amortization
b. Option
c. Annuity
d. AT'T Mobility LLC

19. In corporate finance, _________ analysis applies put option and call option valuation techniques to capital budgeting decisions. A _________ itself, is the right--but not the obligation--to undertake some business decision; typically the option to make, or abandon, a capital investment. For example, the opportunity to invest in the expansion of a firm's factory, or alternatively to sell the factory, is a _________.

a. Cash flow
b. Real option
c. Capital budgeting
d. Book building

20. _________ occurs when an entity that has issued callable bonds calls those debt securities from the debt holders with the express purpose of reissuing new debt at a lower coupon rate. In essence, the issue of new, lower-interest debt allows the company to prematurely refund the older, higher-interest debt.

On the contrary, NonRefundable Bonds may be callable but they cannot be re-issued with a lower coupon rate.

a. Systematic risk
b. No-arbitrage bounds
c. Refunding
d. Market neutral

21. A _________ is a fund established by a government agency or business for the purpose of reducing debt.

The _________ was first used in Great Britain in the 18th century to reduce national debt. While used by Robert Walpole in 1716 and effectively in the 1720s and early 1730s, it originated in the commercial tax syndicates of the Italian peninsula of the 14th century to retire redeemable public debt of those cities.

a. Modern portfolio theory
b. Security interest
c. Debtor
d. Sinking fund

22. In finance, a _________ is a type of bond that can be converted into shares of stock in the issuing company, usually at some pre-announced ratio. It is a hybrid security with debt- and equity-like features. Although it typically has a low coupon rate, the holder is compensated with the ability to convert the bond to common stock, usually at a substantial discount to the stock's market value.

a. Bond fund
b. Gilts
c. Corporate bond
d. Convertible bond

23. _________ are formal records of a business' financial activities.

_________ provide an overview of a business' financial condition in both short and long term. There are four basic _________:

1. **Balance sheet**: also referred to as statement of financial position or condition, reports on a company's assets, liabilities, and net equity as of a given point in time.
2. **Income statement**: also referred to as Profit and Loss statement (or a 'P'L'), reports on a company's income, expenses, and profits over a period of time.
3. **Statement of retained earnings**: explains the changes in a company's retained earnings over the reporting period.
4. **Statement of cash flows**: reports on a company's cash flow activities, particularly its operating, investing and financing activities.

a. Financial statements
b. Statement of retained earnings
c. Notes to the Financial Statements
d. Statement on Auditing Standards No. 70: Service Organizations

24. _________, in accrual accounting, is any account where the asset or liability is not realized until a future date, e.g. annuities, charges, taxes, income, etc. The _________ item may be carried, dependent on type of deferral, as either an asset or liability.See also: accrual

_________ is also used in the university admissions process. It is the action by which a school rejects a student for early admission but still opts to review that student in the general admissions pool.

a. Net profit
b. Current asset
c. Revenue
d. Deferred

25. _________ refers to a business or organization attempting to acquire goods or services to accomplish the goals of the enterprise. Though there are several organizations that attempt to set standards in the _________ process, processes can vary greatly between organizations. Typically the word '_________' is not used interchangeably with the word 'procurement', since procurement typically includes Expediting, Supplier Quality, and Traffic and Logistics (T'L) in addition to _________.

a. Purchasing
b. 4-4-5 Calendar
c. 529 plan
d. 7-Eleven

26. An _________ can be defined as a contract which provides an income stream in return for an initial payment.

An immediate _________ is an _________ for which the time between the contract date and the date of the first payment is not longer than the time interval between payments. A common use for an immediate _________ is to provide a pension to a retired person or persons.

a. Annuity
b. Amortization
c. AT'T Inc.
d. Intrinsic value

27. The _________, effective annual interest rate, Annual Equivalent Rate (AER) or simply effective rate is the interest rate on a loan or financial product restated from the nominal interest rate as an interest rate with annual compound interest. It is used to compare the annual interest between loans with different compounding terms (daily, monthly, annually, or other.)

The _________ differs in two important respects from the annual percentage rate (APR):

1. the _________ generally does not incorporate one-time charges such as front-end fees;
2. the _________ is (generally) not defined by legal or regulatory authorities (as APR is in many jurisdictions.)

By contrast, the 'effective APR' is used as a legal term, where front-fees and other costs can be included, as defined by local law.

Annual Percentage Yield or effective annual yield is the analogous concept used for savings or investment products, such as a certificate of deposit.

a. AAB
b. Effective interest rate
c. A Random Walk Down Wall Street
d. ABN Amro

28. _________ is a company's earnings per share (EPS) calculated using fully diluted shares outstanding (i.e. including the impact of stock option grants and convertible bonds.) Diluted EPS indicates a 'worst case' scenario, one in which everyone who could have received stock without purchasing it directly for the full market value did so.

To find diluted EPS, basic EPS is calculated for each of the categories on the income statement first.

a. Financial ratio
b. Net assets
c. Price/cash flow ratio
d. Diluted Earnings Per Share

29. The _________ is a private, not-for-profit organization whose primary purpose is to develop generally accepted accounting principles (GAAP) within the United States in the public's interest. The Securities and Exchange Commission (SEC) designated the _________ as the organization responsible for setting accounting standards for public companies in the U.S. It was created in 1973, replacing the Accounting Principles Board and the Committee on Accounting Procedure of the American Institute of Certified Public Accountants. The _________'s mission is 'to establish and improve standards of financial accounting and reporting for the guidance and education of the public, including issuers, auditors, and users of financial information.'

The _________ is not a governmental body.

a. Credit karma
b. FASB
c. MRU Holdings
d. PlaNet Finance

30. A _________ is a document that indicates that the bearer of the document has title to property, such as shares or bonds. They differ from normal registered instruments, in that no records are kept of who owns the underlying property, or of the transactions involving transfer of ownership. Whoever physically holds the bearer bond papers owns the property.

a. Book entry
b. Bearer instrument
c. Marketable
d. Securities lending

31. A _________ is different from normal stock in that it is unregistered - no records are kept of the owner, or the transactions involving ownership. Whoever physically holds the _________ papers owns the stock or corporation. This is useful for investors and corporate officers who wish to retain anonymity.

a. Revenue bonds
b. Clean price
c. Bearer bond
d. Gilts

32. A _________ is defined as a certificate of agreement of loans which is given under the company's stamp and carries an undertaking that the _________ holder will get a fixed return (fixed on the basis of interest rates) and the principal amount whenever the _________ matures.

In finance, a _________ is a long-term debt instrument used by governments and large companies to obtain funds. It is defined as 'a debt secured only by the debtor's earning power, not by a lien on any specific asset.' It is similar to a bond except the securitization conditions are different.

a. Collateral Management
b. Collection agency
c. Partial Payment
d. Debenture

33. Companies that have publicly traded securities typically use _________ to keep track of the individuals and entities that own their stocks and bonds. Most _________ are banks or trust companies, but sometimes a company acts as its own transfer agent.

_________ perform three main functions:

1. Issue and cancel certificates to reflect changes in ownership. For example, when a company declares a stock dividend or stock split, the transfer agent issues new shares. _________ keep records of who owns a company's stocks and bonds and how those stocks and bonds are held--whether by the owner in certificate form, by the company in book-entry form, or by the investor's brokerage firm in street name. They also keep records of how many shares or bonds each investor owns.
2. Act as an intermediary for the company. A transfer agent may also serve as the company's paying agent to pay out interest, cash and stock dividends, or other distributions to stock- and bondholders. In addition, _________ act as proxy agent (sending out proxy materials), exchange agent (exchanging a company's stock or bonds in a merger), tender agent (tendering shares in a tender offer), and mailing agent (mailing the company's quarterly, annual, and other reports.)
3. Handle lost, destroyed, or stolen certificates. _________ help shareholders and bondholders when a stock or bond certificate has been lost, destroyed, or stolen.

In many cases, you can find out which transfer agent a company uses by visiting the investor relations section of the company's website.

a. 7-Eleven
b. 529 plan
c. Transfer agents
d. 4-4-5 Calendar

34. A _________ is a fungible, negotiable instrument representing financial value. They are broadly categorized into debt securities (such as banknotes, bonds and debentures), and equity securities; e.g., common stocks. The company or other entity issuing the _________ is called the issuer.

a. Book entry
b. Securities lending
c. Tracking stock
d. Security

35. The institution most often referenced by the word '_________' is a public or publicly traded _________, the shares of which are traded on a public stock exchange (e.g., the New York Stock Exchange or Nasdaq in the United States) where shares of stock of _________s are bought and sold by and to the general public. Most of the largest businesses in the world are publicly traded _________s. However, the majority of _________s are said to be closely held, privately held or close _________s, meaning that no ready market exists for the trading of shares.

a. Depository Trust Company
b. Protect
c. Federal Home Loan Mortgage Corporation
d. Corporation

36. In finance, _________ occurs when a debtor has not met its legal obligations according to the debt contract, e.g. it has not made a scheduled payment, or has violated a loan covenant (condition) of the debt contract. _________ may occur if the debtor is either unwilling or unable to pay their debt. This can occur with all debt obligations including bonds, mortgages, loans, and promissory notes.

a. Credit crunch
b. Debt validation
c. Vendor finance
d. Default

37. _________ is the risk of loss due to a debtor's non-payment of a loan or other line of credit (either the principal or interest (coupon) or both)

Most lenders employ their own models (credit scorecards) to rank potential and existing customers according to risk, and then apply appropriate strategies. With products such as unsecured personal loans or mortgages, lenders charge a higher price for higher risk customers and vice versa. With revolving products such as credit cards and overdrafts, risk is controlled through careful setting of credit limits.

a. Liquidity risk
b. Market risk
c. Transaction risk
d. Credit risk

38. In finance, a _________ (non-investment grade bond, speculative grade bond or junk bond) is a bond that is rated below investment grade at the time of purchase. These bonds have a higher risk of default or other adverse credit events, but typically pay higher yields than better quality bonds in order to make them attractive to investors.

a. Volatility
b. Private equity
c. Sharpe ratio
d. High yield bond

39. In finance, _________, frequently issued in the form of a senior note, is debt that takes priority over other unsecured debt owed by the issuer. _________ has greater seniority in the issuer's capital structure than subordinated debt. In the event the issuer goes bankrupt, _________ theoretically must be repaid before other creditors receive any payment.

a. Zero-coupon bond
b. Bond fund
c. Bond option
d. Senior debt

40. In finance, _________ is debt which ranks after other debts should a company fall into receivership or be closed.

Such debt is referred to as subordinate, because the debt providers have subordinate status in relationship to the normal debt. A typical example for this would be when a promoter of a company invests money in the form of debt, rather than in the form of stock.

a. Credit rating
b. Cross-collateralization
c. Subordinated debt
d. Participation loan

41. _________ is that which is owed; usually referencing assets owed, but the term can cover other obligations. In the case of assets, _________ is a means of using future purchasing power in the present before a summation has been earned. Some companies and corporations use _________ as a part of their overall corporate finance strategy.

a. Partial Payment
b. Debt
c. Credit cycle
d. Cross-collateralization

42. _________ is a list for goods and materials held available in stock by a business. It is also used for a list of the contents of a household and for a list for testamentary purposes of the possessions of someone who has died. In accounting _________ is considered an asset.

a. AAB
b. A Random Walk Down Wall Street
c. ABN Amro
d. Inventory

43. A bond is considered _________ if its credit rating is BBB- or higher by Standard and Poor's or Baa3 or higher by Moody's or BBB(low) or higher by DBRS. Generally they are bonds that are judged by the rating agency as likely enough to meet payment obligations that banks are allowed to invest in them.

Ratings play a critical role in determining how much companies and other entities that issue debt, including sovereign governments, have to pay to access credit markets, i.e., the amount of interest they pay on their issued debt.

a. ABN Amro
b. A Random Walk Down Wall Street
c. AAB
d. Investment grade

44. In finance, _________ (or gearing) is borrowing money to supplement existing funds for investment in such a way that the potential positive or negative outcome is magnified and/or enhanced. It generally refers to using borrowed funds, or debt, so as to attempt to increase the returns to equity. Deleveraging is the action of reducing borrowings.

a. Financial endowment
b. Limited partnership
c. Pension fund
d. Leverage

45. _________ (also trust indenture or deed of trust) is a legal document issued to lenders and describes key terms such as the interest rate, maturity date, convertibility, pledge, promises, representations, covenants, and other terms of the bond offering. When the Offering Memorandum is prepared in advance of marketing a Bond, the indenture will typically be summarised in the 'Description of Notes' section.

a. Court of Audit of Belgium
b. Fair Labor Standards Act
c. McFadden Act
d. Bond indenture

46. _________ is the removal or simplification of government rules and regulations that constrain the operation of market forces. _________ does not mean elimination of laws against fraud, but eliminating or reducing government control of how business is done, thereby moving toward a more free market.

The stated rationale for '_________' is often that fewer and simpler regulations will lead to a raised level of competitiveness, therefore higher productivity, more efficiency and lower prices overall.

a. Deregulation
b. Demand shock
c. Value added
d. Supply shock

47. In economics, _________ is a measure of the relative satisfaction from or desirability of consumption of various goods and services. Given this measure, one may speak meaningfully of increasing or decreasing _________, and thereby explain economic behavior in terms of attempts to increase one's _________. For illustrative purposes, changes in _________ are sometimes expressed in units called utils.

a. AAB
b. Utility function
c. A Random Walk Down Wall Street
d. Utility

48. _________ or financing is to provide capital (funds), which means money for a project, a person, a business or any other private or public institutions.

Those funds can be allocated for either short term or long term purposes. The health fund is a new way of _________ private healthcare centers.

a. Product life cycle
b. Funding
c. Proxy fight
d. Synthetic CDO

49. _________ is a process by which a firm can obtain the use of a certain fixed assets for which it must pay a series of contractual, periodic, tax deductable payments. The lessee is the receiver of the services or the assets under the lease contract and the lessor is the owner of the assets. The relationship between the tenant and the landlord is called a tenancy, and can be for a fixed or an indefinite period of time (called the term of the lease).

a. Quiet period
b. Foreign Corrupt Practices Act
c. Royalties
d. Leasing

50. _________ usually means an asset or debt or financing activity not on the company's balance sheet. It could involve a lease or a separate subsidiary or a contingent liability such as a letter of credit. It also involves loan commitments, futures, forwards and other derivatives except such derivatives pertaining to equity securities, ESOP, or phantom stock, which usually must be held as reserves in the Long Term Debt section of a Balance Sheet (.

a. AAB
b. A Random Walk Down Wall Street
c. ABN Amro
d. Off balance sheet

51. In financial accounting, a _________ or statement of financial position is a summary of a person's or organization's balances. Assets, liabilities and ownership equity are listed as of a specific date, such as the end of its financial year. A _________ is often described as a snapshot of a company's financial condition.

a. Financial statements
b. Statement of retained earnings
c. Statement on Auditing Standards No. 70: Service Organizations
d. Balance sheet

52. The role of the _________ is to issue accounting standards in the United Kingdom. It is recognised for that purpose under the Companies Act 1985. It took over the task of setting accounting standards from the Accounting Standards Committee (ASC) in 1990.

a. Accounting Standards Board
b. AAB
c. A Random Walk Down Wall Street
d. ABN Amro

53. A finance lease or _________ is a type of lease. It is a commercial arrangement where:

- the lessee (customer or borrower) will select an asset (equipment, vehicle, software);
- the lessor (finance company) will purchase that asset;
- the lessee will have use of that asset during the lease;
- the lessee will pay a series of rentals or installments for the use of that asset;
- the lessor will recover a large part or all of the cost of the asset plus earn interest from the rentals paid by the lessee;
- the lessee has the option to acquire ownership of the asset (e.g. paying the last rental, or bargain option purchase price);

The finance company is the legal owner of the asset during duration of the lease.

However the lessee has control over the asset providing them the benefits and risks of (economic) ownership.

A finance lease differs from an operating lease in that:

- in a finance lease the lessee has use of the asset over most of its economic life and beyond (generally by making small 'peppercorn' payments at the end of the lease term.)

In an operating lease the lessee only uses the asset for some of the asset's life.

- in a finance lease the lessor will recover all or most of the cost of the equipment from the rentals paid by the lessee.

In an operating lease the lessor will have a substantial investment or residual value on completion of the lease.

- in a finance lease the lessee has the benefits and risks of economic ownership of the asset (e.g. risk of obsolescence, paying for maintenance, claiming capital allowances/depreciation.)

In an operating lease the lessor has the benefits and risks of owning the asset.

The U.S. Financial Accounting Standards Board and the International Accounting Standards Board announced in 2006 a joint project to comprehensively review lease accounting standards.

a. Capitalization rate	b. Cash management
c. Capital lease	d. Cash concentration

54. _________ is the field of accountancy concerned with the preparation of financial statements for decision makers, such as stockholders, suppliers, banks, employees, government agencies, owners, and other stakeholders. The fundamental need for _________ is to reduce principal-agent problem by measuring and monitoring agents' performance and reporting the results to interested users.

_________ is used to prepare accounting information for people outside the organization or not involved in the day to day running of the company.

a. 4-4-5 Calendar	b. 7-Eleven
c. Financial Accounting	d. 529 plan

55. The _________ is a private, not-for-profit organization whose primary purpose is to develop generally accepted accounting principles (GAAP) within the United States in the public's interest. The Securities and Exchange Commission (SEC) designated the _________ as the organization responsible for setting accounting standards for public companies in the U.S. It was created in 1973, replacing the Accounting Principles Board and the Committee on Accounting Procedure of the American Institute of Certified Public Accountants. The _________'s mission is 'to establish and improve standards of financial accounting and reporting for the guidance and education of the public, including issuers, auditors, and users of financial information.'

The _________ is not a governmental body.

a. KPMG
b. Federal Deposit Insurance Corporation
c. Financial Accounting Standards Board
d. World Congress of Accountants

56. An _________ is a lease whose term is short compared to the useful life of the asset or piece of equipment (an airliner, a ship etc.) being leased. An _________ is commonly used to acquire equipment on a relatively short-term basis.

a. ABN Amro
b. A Random Walk Down Wall Street
c. Operating lease
d. AAB

57. Leasing is a process by which a firm can obtain the use of a certain fixed assets for which it must pay a series of contractual, periodic, tax deductable payments. The lessee is the receiver of the services or the assets under the lease contract and the lessor is the owner of the assets. The relationship between the tenant and the landlord is called a _________, and can be for a fixed or an indefinite period of time (called the term of the lease.)

a. Real Estate Investment Trust
b. Tenancy
c. REIT
d. Real estate investing

58. _________ is one of the constituents of a leasing calculus or operation. It describes the future value of a good in terms of percentage of depreciation of its initial value.

Example: A car is sold at a list price of $20,000 today. After a usage of 36 months and 50,000 miles its value is contractually defined as 50% or $10,000. The credited amount, on which the interest is applied, thus is $20,000 present value minus $10,000 future value.

a. Net pay
b. Round-tripping
c. Residual value
d. Days Sales Outstanding

59. _________ is the provision of resources (such as granting a loan) by one party to another party where that second party does not reimburse the first party immediately, thereby generating a debt, and instead arranges either to repay or return those resources (or material(s) of equal value) at a later date. The first party is called a creditor, also known as a lender, while the second party is called a debtor, also known as a borrower.

Movements of financial capital are normally dependent on either _________ or equity transfers.

a. Credit
b. Warrant
c. Comparable
d. Clearing house

60. _________ short for sale-and-_________ is a financial transaction, where one sells an asset and leases it back for a long-term: thus one continues to be able to use the asset, but no longer owns it.

This is generally done for fixed assets, notably real estate and planes, and the purposes are varied, but include financing, accounting, and tax reasons.

After purchasing an asset, the owner enters a long-term agreement by which the property is leased back to the seller, at an agreed-to rate.

a. 529 plan
b. Leaseback,
c. 4-4-5 Calendar
d. 7-Eleven

61. _________ is a measure of the ability of a debtor to pay their debts as and when they fall due. It is usually expressed as a ratio or a percentage of current liabilities.

For a corporation with a published balance sheet there are various ratios used to calculate a measure of liquidity.

a. Operating profit margin
b. Accounting liquidity
c. Invested capital
d. Operating leverage

62. In economics, business, and accounting, a _________ is the value of money that has been used up to produce something, and hence is not available for use anymore. In business, the _________ may be one of acquisition, in which case the amount of money expended to acquire it is counted as _________. In this case, money is the input that is gone in order to acquire the thing.

a. Marginal cost
b. Fixed costs
c. Sliding scale fees
d. Cost

63. A _________ is a lease in which the lessor puts up some of the money required to purchase the asset and borrows the rest from a lender. The lender is given a senior secured interest on the asset and an assignment of the lease and lease payments. The lessee makes payments to the lessor, who makes payments to the lender.

a. Collection agency
b. Leveraged lease
c. Guaranteed consumer funding
d. Debt buyer

1. _________ is a form of corporation equity ownership represented in the securities. It is dangerous in comparison to preferred shares and some other investment options, in that in the event of bankruptcy, _________ investors receive their funds after preferred stockholders, bondholders, creditors, etc. On the other hand, common shares on average perform better than preferred shares or bonds over time.

a. Stock split
b. Common stock
c. Stop-limit order
d. Stock market bubble

2. _________ is an estimate of the fair value of corporations and their stocks, by using fundamental economic criteria. This theoretical valuation has to be perfected with market criteria, as the final purpose is to determine potential market prices.

a. Growth stocks
b. Security Analysis
c. 4-4-5 Calendar
d. Stock valuation

3. In mathematics, _________ are used in the study of chance and probability. They were developed to assist in the analysis of games of chance, stochastic events, and the results of scientific experiments by capturing only the mathematical properties necessary to answer probabilistic questions. Further formalizations have firmly grounded the entity in the theoretical domains of mathematics by making use of measure theory.

a. Random variables
b. Monte Carlo methods
c. Standard deviation
d. Variance

4. In finance, _________, also known as return on investment is the ratio of money gained or lost on an investment relative to the amount of money invested. The amount of money gained or lost may be referred to as interest, profit/loss, gain/loss, or net income/loss. The money invested may be referred to as the asset, capital, principal, or the cost basis of the investment.

a. Composiition of Creditors
b. Stock or scrip dividends
c. Doctrine of the Proper Law
d. Rate of return

5. In finance, _________ is the process of estimating the potential market value of a financial asset or liability. they can be done on assets (for example, investments in marketable securities such as stocks, options, business enterprises, or intangible assets such as patents and trademarks) or on liabilities (e.g., Bonds issued by a company.) _________s are required in many contexts including investment analysis, capital budgeting, merger and acquisition transactions, financial reporting, taxable events to determine the proper tax liability, and in litigation.

a. Share
b. Margin
c. Procter ' Gamble
d. Valuation

6. A _________ is a profit that results from investments into a capital asset, such as stocks, bonds or real estate, which exceeds the purchase price. It is the difference between a higher selling price and a lower purchase price, resulting in a financial gain for the seller. Conversely, a capital loss arises if the proceeds from the sale of a capital asset are less than the purchase price.

a. Tax brackets
b. Payroll tax
c. Capital gains tax
d. Capital gain

7. A _________ is a payment made by a corporation to its shareholder members. When a corporation earns a profit or surplus, that money can be put to two uses: it can either be re-invested in the business (called retained earnings), or it can be paid to the shareholders as a _________. Many corporations retain a portion of their earnings and pay the remainder as a _________.

a. Dividend puzzle
b. Dividend yield
c. Dividend
d. Special dividend

8. The _________ on a company stock is the company's annual dividend payments divided by its market cap, or the dividend per share divided by the price per share. It is often expressed as a percentage.

Dividend payments on preferred shares are stipulated by the prospectus.

a. Special dividend
b. Dividend imputation
c. Dividend reinvestment plan
d. Dividend yield

9. In finance, the term _________ describes the amount in cash that returns to the owners of a security. Normally it does not include the price variations, at the difference of the total return. _________ applies to various stated rates of return on stocks (common and preferred, and convertible), fixed income instruments (bonds, notes, bills, strips, zero coupon), and some other investment type insurance products (e.g. annuities.)

a. Macaulay duration
b. Yield
c. 4-4-5 Calendar
d. Yield to maturity

10. _________ is the balance of the amounts of cash being received and paid by a business during a defined period of time, sometimes tied to a specific project. Measurement of _________ can be used

- to evaluate the state or performance of a business or project.
- to determine problems with liquidity. Being profitable does not necessarily mean being liquid. A company can fail because of a shortage of cash, even while profitable.
- to generate project rate of returns. The time of _________s into and out of projects are used as inputs to financial models such as internal rate of return, and net present value.
- to examine income or growth of a business when it is believed that accrual accounting concepts do not represent economic realities. Alternately, _________ can be used to 'validate' the net income generated by accrual accounting.

_________ as a generic term may be used differently depending on context, and certain _________ definitions may be adapted by analysts and users for their own uses. Common terms include operating _________ and free _________.

_________s can be classified into:

1. Operational _________s: Cash received or expended as a result of the company's core business activities.
2. Investment _________s: Cash received or expended through capital expenditure, investments or acquisitions.
3. Financing _________s: Cash received or expended as a result of financial activities, such as interests and dividends.

All three together - the net _________ - are necessary to reconcile the beginning cash balance to the ending cash balance. Loan draw downs or equity injections, that is just shifting of capital but no expenditure as such, are not considered in the net _________.

a. Shareholder value
b. Corporate finance
c. Real option
d. Cash flow

11. In finance, a _________ is a debt security, in which the authorized issuer owes the holders a debt and, depending on the terms of the _________, is obliged to pay interest (the coupon) and/or to repay the principal at a later date, termed maturity.

Thus a _________ is a loan: the issuer is the borrower, the _________ holder is the lender, and the coupon is the interest. _________s provide the borrower with external funds to finance long-term investments, or, in the case of government _________s, to finance current expenditure.

a. Puttable bond
b. Bond
c. Convertible bond
d. Catastrophe bonds

12. _________ is the value on a given date of a future payment or series of future payments, discounted to reflect the time value of money and other factors such as investment risk. _________ calculations are widely used in business and economics to provide a means to compare cash flows at different times on a meaningful 'like to like' basis.

The most commonly applied model of the time value of money is compound interest.

a. Present value
b. Present value of benefits
c. Negative gearing
d. Net present value

13. _________ of a business involves analyzing its financial statements and health, its management and competitive advantages, and its competitors and markets. The term is used to distinguish such analysis from other types of investment analysis, such as quantitative analysis and technical analysis.

_________ is performed on historical and present data, but with the goal of making financial forecasts.

a. Stock valuation
b. Growth stocks
c. Fundamental analysis
d. 4-4-5 Calendar

14. In finance, _________ refers to the value of a security which is intrinsic to or contained in the security itself. It is also frequently called fundamental value. It is ordinarily calculated by summing the future income generated by the asset, and discounting it to the present value.

a. Amortization
b. Intrinsic value
c. Accretion
d. Alpha

15. _________ is an economic concept with commonplace familiarity. It is the price that a good or service is offered at, or will fetch, in the marketplace. It is of interest mainly in the study of microeconomics.

a. Central Securities Depository
b. Convertible arbitrage
c. Market price
d. Delta hedging

16. _________ is a variant of the Discounted cash flow model, a method for valuing a stock or business. Often used to provide difficult-to-resolve valuation issues for litigation, tax planning, and business transactions that are currently off market.

It assumes that the company issues a dividend that has a current value of D that grows at a constant rate g. It also assumes that the required rate of return for the stock remains constant at k which is equal to the cost of equity for that company. It involves summing the infinite series which gives the value of price current P.

a. Stock or scrip dividends
b. Special journals
c. Securitization
d. Gordon growth model

17. _________ is a theory that all economic activities and policies should be oriented towards achieving a state of equilibrium, a steady state.

The theory asserts that the continuous growth model is inherently unstable resulting in a 'boom/bust' cycle, and that continuous growth in the context of finite resources is unlikely to support current levels of prosperity indefinitely.

Proponents of this theory also explicitly challenge the popular equation of economic growth with progress - an equation they have labelled Growth Fetish - and posit that sustainability has inherent value.

a. Zero growth
b. 7-Eleven
c. 529 plan
d. 4-4-5 Calendar

18. The phrase _________ refers to the aspect of corporate strategy, corporate finance and management dealing with the buying, selling and combining of different companies that can aid, finance, or help a growing company in a given industry grow rapidly without having to create another business entity.

An acquisition, also known as a takeover, is the buying of one company (the 'target') by another. An acquisition may be friendly or hostile.

a. 529 plan
b. 4-4-5 Calendar
c. 7-Eleven
d. Mergers and acquisitions

19. In financial and business accounting, _________ is a measure of a firm's profitability that excludes interest and income tax expenses.

EBIT = Operating Revenue - Operating Expenses (OPEX) + Non-operating Income

Operating Income = Operating Revenue - Operating Expenses

Operating income is the difference between operating revenues and operating expenses, but it is also sometimes used as a synonym for EBIT and operating profit. This is true if the firm has no non-operating income.

a. ABN Amro
b. A Random Walk Down Wall Street
c. AAB
d. Earnings before interest and taxes

20. A _________ is an annuity in which the periodic payments begin on a fixed date and continue indefinitely. It is sometimes referred to as a perpetual annuity. Fixed coupon payments on permanently invested (irredeemable) sums of money are prime examples of these. Scholarships paid perpetually from an endowment fit the definition of _________.

a. Stochastic volatility
b. LIBOR market model
c. Current yield
d. Perpetuity

21. A _________ rocket is a rocket that uses two or more stages, each of which contains its own engines and propellant. A tandem or serial stage is mounted on top of another stage; a parallel stage is attached alongside another stage. The result is effectively two or more rockets stacked on top of or attached next to each other.

a. Multistage
b. 4-4-5 Calendar
c. 7-Eleven
d. 529 plan

22. _________ is the process of determining the fair price of a bond. As with any security or capital investment, the fair value of a bond is the present value of the stream of cash flows it is expected to generate. Hence, the price or value of a bond is determined by discounting the bond's expected cash flows to the present using the appropriate discount rate.

a. Bond valuation
b. Bond fund
c. Catastrophe bonds
d. Collateralized debt obligations

23. In business and finance, a _________ (also referred to as equity _________) of stock means a _________ of ownership in a corporation (company.) In the plural, stocks is often used as a synonym for _________s especially in the United States, but it is less commonly used that way outside of North America.

In the United Kingdom, South Africa, and Australia, stock can also refer to completely different financial instruments such as government bonds or, less commonly, to all kinds of marketable securities.

a. Bucket shop
b. Margin
c. Share
d. Procter ' Gamble

24. _________ is the imposition of two or more taxes on the same income (in the case of income taxes), asset (in the case of capital taxes), or financial transaction (in the case of sales taxes.) It refers to two distinct situations:

- taxation of dividend income without relief or credit for taxes paid by the company paying the dividend on the income from which the dividend is paid. This arises in the so-called 'classical' system of corporate taxation, used in the United States.
- taxation by two or more countries of the same income, asset or transaction, for example income paid by an entity of one country to a resident of a different country. The double liability is often mitigated by tax treaties between countries.

It is not unusual for a business or individual who is resident in one country to make a taxable gain (earnings, profits) in another. This person may find that he is obliged by domestic laws to pay tax on that gain locally and pay again in the country in which the gain was made. Since this is inequitable, many nations make bilateral _________ agreements with each other.

a. 529 plan
b. 4-4-5 Calendar
c. 7-Eleven
d. Double taxation

25. _________ generally refers to the buying and holding of shares of stock on a stock market by individuals and funds in anticipation of income from dividends and capital gain as the value of the stock rises. It also sometimes refers to the acquisition of equity (ownership) participation in a private (unlisted) company or a startup (a company being created or newly created.) When the investment is in infant companies, it is referred to as venture capital investing and is generally understood to be higher risk than investment in listed going-concern situations.

a. Intellidex
b. Open outcry
c. Insider trading
d. Equity investment

26. A _________ is a right to acquire certain property in preference to any other person. It usually refers to property newly coming into existence. A right to acquire existing property in preference to any other person is usually referred to as a right of first refusal.

In practice, the most common form of _________ is the right of existing shareholders to acquire newly issued shares issued by a company in a rights issue, a usually but not always public offering.

a. Down payment
b. Court of Audit of Belgium
c. Fraud deterrence
d. Pre-emption right

27. The _________ is a stock exchange based in New York City, New York. It is the largest stock exchange in the world by dollar value of its listed companies securities. As of October 2008, the combined capitalization of all domestic _________ listed companies was $10.1 trillion.

a. 529 plan
b. 4-4-5 Calendar
c. 7-Eleven
d. New York Stock Exchange

28. A _________, securities exchange or (in Europe) bourse is a corporation or mutual organization which provides 'trading' facilities for stock brokers and traders, to trade stocks and other securities. _________s also provide facilities for the issue and redemption of securities as well as other financial instruments and capital events including the payment of income and dividends. The securities traded on a _________ include: shares issued by companies, unit trusts and other pooled investment products and bonds.

a. 4-4-5 Calendar
b. 529 plan
c. 7-Eleven
d. Stock Exchange

29. An _________ is a contract written by a seller that conveys to the buyer the right -- but not the obligation -- to buy (in the case of a call _________) or to sell (in the case of a put _________) a particular asset, such as a piece of property such as, among others, a futures contract. In return for granting the _________, the seller collects a payment (the premium) from the buyer.

For example, buying a call _________ provides the right to buy a specified quantity of a security at a set strike price at some time on or before expiration, while buying a put _________ provides the right to sell.

a. Annuity
b. Option
c. AT'T Mobility LLC
d. Amortization

30. The _________ is the current method of accelerated asset depreciation required by the United States income tax code. Under _________, all assets are divided into classes which dictate the number of years over which an asset's cost will be recovered.

Prior to the Accelerated Cost Recovery System (ACRS), most capital purchases were depreciated using a straight line technique, that allowed for the depreciation of the asset over its useful life.

a. 4-4-5 Calendar
b. 529 plan
c. 7-Eleven
d. Modified Accelerated Cost Recovery System

31. In economics, business, and accounting, a _________ is the value of money that has been used up to produce something, and hence is not available for use anymore. In business, the _________ may be one of acquisition, in which case the amount of money expended to acquire it is counted as _________. In this case, money is the input that is gone in order to acquire the thing.

a. Fixed costs
b. Marginal cost
c. Sliding scale fees
d. Cost

32. _________ is a multiple-winner voting system intended to promote proportional representation while also being simple to understand.

_________ is used frequently in corporate governance, where it is mandated by many U.S. states, and it was used to elect the Illinois House of Representatives from 1870 until its repeal in 1980. It was used in England in the late 19th century to elect school boards.

a. 529 plan
b. Cumulative voting
c. 4-4-5 Calendar
d. 7-Eleven

33. _________, refers to consumption opportunity gained by an entity within a specified time frame, which is generally expressed in monetary terms. However, for households and individuals, '_________ is the sum of all the wages, salaries, profits, interests payments, rents and other forms of earnings received... in a given period of time.' For firms, _________ generally refers to net-profit: what remains of revenue after expenses have been subtracted.

a. OIBDA
b. Annual report
c. Accrual
d. Income

34. In business and accounting, _________s are everything of value that is owned by a person or company. The balance sheet of a firm records the monetary value of the _________s owned by the firm. The two major _________ classes are tangible _________s and intangible _________s.

a. Accounts payable
b. EBITDA
c. Income
d. Asset

35. _________ is typically a higher ranking stock than voting shares, and its terms are negotiated between the corporation and the investor.

_________ usually carry no voting rights, but may carry superior priority over common stock in the payment of dividends and upon liquidation. _________ may carry a dividend that is paid out prior to any dividends to common stock holders.

a. Trade-off theory
b. Preferred stock
c. Follow-on offering
d. Second lien loan

36. _________ is a life of security. It may also refer to the final payment date of a loan or other financial instrument, at which point all remaining interest and principal is due to be paid.

1, 3, 6 months _________ band can be calculated by using 30-day per month periods.

a. Replacement cost
b. False billing
c. Primary market
d. Maturity

37. A _________ is a fungible, negotiable instrument representing financial value. They are broadly categorized into debt securities (such as banknotes, bonds and debentures), and equity securities; e.g., common stocks. The company or other entity issuing the _________ is called the issuer.

a. Securities lending
b. Tracking stock
c. Security
d. Book entry

38. _________ is a legally declared inability or impairment of ability of an individual or organization to pay their creditors. Creditors may file a _________ petition against a debtor ('involuntary _________') in an effort to recoup a portion of what they are owed or initiate a restructuring. In the majority of cases, however, _________ is initiated by the debtor (a 'voluntary _________' that is filed by the bankrupt individual or organization.)

a. 529 plan
b. 4-4-5 Calendar
c. Debt settlement
d. Bankruptcy

39. A _________ or a stock investor is an individual or firm who buys and sells stocks or bonds (and possibly other financial assets) in the financial markets. Charting is the use of graphical and analytical patterns and data to attempt to predict future prices.

Individuals or firms trading equity (stock) on the stock markets as their principal capacity are called _________s. Stock traders usually try to profit from short-term price volatility with trades lasting anywhere from several seconds to several weeks.

a. Lookback options
b. Stock trader
c. Rate of return
d. Stock or scrip dividends

40. _________ is a security analysis discipline for forecasting the future direction of prices through the study of past market data, primarily price and volume. In its purest form, _________ considers only the actual price and volume behavior of the market or instrument. Technical analysts may employ models and trading rules based on price and volume transformations, such as the relative strength index, moving averages, regressions, inter-market and intra-market price correlations, cycles or, classically, through recognition of chart patterns.

a. Dow theory
b. Support and resistance
c. Point and figure
d. Technical analysis

41. A _________ is a financial contract between two parties, the buyer and the seller of this type of option. Often it is simply labeled a 'call'. The buyer of the option has the right, but not the obligation to buy an agreed quantity of a particular commodity or financial instrument (the underlying instrument) from the seller of the option at a certain time (the expiration date) for a certain price (the strike price.)

a. Bear call spread
b. Bull spread
c. Bear spread
d. Call option

42. A _________ is a financial contract whose value is derived from the value of something else (known as the underlying.) The underlying on which a _________ is based can be an asset, weather conditions bonds or other forms of credit.

a. 529 plan
b. 7-Eleven
c. 4-4-5 Calendar
d. Derivative

43. In options, the _________ is a key variable in a derivatives contract between two parties. Where the contract requires delivery of the underlying instrument, the trade will be at the _________, regardless of the spot price (market price) of the underlying instrument at that time.

Definition - The fixed price at which the owner of an option can purchase, in the case of a call in the case of a put, the underlying security or commodity.

a. Strike price
b. Swaption
c. Naked put
d. Moneyness

44. In finance, _________ (or gearing) is borrowing money to supplement existing funds for investment in such a way that the potential positive or negative outcome is magnified and/or enhanced. It generally refers to using borrowed funds, or debt, so as to attempt to increase the returns to equity. Deleveraging is the action of reducing borrowings.

a. Leverage
b. Financial endowment
c. Limited partnership
d. Pension fund

45. _________ is a term used to describe any option trading strategy that involves selling options. An option writer sells options to potentially profit from the decline of extrinsic value on options, sometimes referred to as time value.

_________ strategies include covered calls, naked calls and naked puts, bear call spreads, bull put spreads, ratio credit spreads, short strangles and short straddles.

a. ABN Amro
b. AAB
c. A Random Walk Down Wall Street
d. Options writing

46. _________ most frequently refers to the standard deviation of the continuously compounded returns of a financial instrument with a specific time horizon. It is often used to quantify the risk of the instrument over that time period. _________ is typically expressed in annualized terms, and it may either be an absolute number ($5) or a fraction of the mean (5%).

a. Volatility
b. Portfolio insurance
c. Seasoned equity offering
d. Currency swap

47. A _________ is a financial contract between two parties, the seller (writer) and the buyer of the option. The put allows its buyer the right but not the obligation to sell a commodity or financial instrument (the underlying instrument) to the writer (seller) of the option at a certain time for a certain price (the strike price.) The writer (seller) has the obligation to purchase the underlying asset at that strike price, if the buyer exercises the option.

a. Bear spread
b. Bear call spread
c. Debit spread
d. Put option

48. The term _________ refers to three closely related concepts:

- The _________ model is a mathematical model of the market for an equity, in which the equity's price is a stochastic process.
- The _________ PDE is a partial differential equation which (in the model) must be satisfied by the price of a derivative on the equity.
- The _________ formula is the result obtained by solving the _________ PDE for a European call option.

Fischer Black and Myron Scholes first articulated the _________ formula in their 1973 paper, 'The Pricing of Options and Corporate Liabilities.' The foundation for their research relied on work developed by scholars such as Jack L. Treynor, Paul Samuelson, A. James Boness, Sheen T. Kassouf, and Edward O. Thorp. The fundamental insight of _________ is that the option is implicitly priced if the stock is traded.

Robert C. Merton was the first to publish a paper expanding the mathematical understanding of the options pricing model and coined the term '_________' options pricing model.

a. Perpetuity
b. Stochastic volatility
c. Modified Internal Rate of Return
d. Black-Scholes

49. The _________ is the financial market where previously issued securities and financial instruments such as stock, bonds, options, and futures are bought and sold. The term '_________' is also used refer to the market for any used goods or assets, or an alternative use for an existing product or asset where the customer base is the second market

With primary issuances of securities or financial instruments, or the primary market, investors purchase these securities directly from issuers such as corporations issuing shares in an IPO or private placement, or directly from the federal government in the case of treasuries.

a. Performance attribution
b. Financial market
c. Delta neutral
d. Secondary market

50. In finance, a _________ is a security that entitles the holder to buy stock of the company that issued it at a specified price, which is usually higher than the stock price at time of issue.

_________s are frequently attached to bonds or preferred stock as a sweetener, allowing the issuer to pay lower interest rates or dividends. They can be used to enhance the yield of the bond, and make them more attractive to potential buyers.

a. Credit
b. Clearing house
c. Warrant
d. Clearing

51. An _________ is a call option on the common stock of a company, issued as a form of non-cash compensation. Restrictions on the option (such as vesting and limited transferability) attempt to align the holder's interest with those of the business' shareholders. If the company's stock rises, holders of options experience a direct financial benefit.

a. Internal financing
b. Underwriting contract
c. Operating ratio
d. Employee Stock option

52. The institution most often referenced by the word '_________' is a public or publicly traded _________, the shares of which are traded on a public stock exchange (e.g., the New York Stock Exchange or Nasdaq in the United States) where shares of stock of _________s are bought and sold by and to the general public. Most of the largest businesses in the world are publicly traded _________s. However, the majority of _________s are said to be closely held, privately held or close _________s, meaning that no ready market exists for the trading of shares.

a. Protect
b. Depository Trust Company
c. Federal Home Loan Mortgage Corporation
d. Corporation

1. _________ is that which is owed; usually referencing assets owed, but the term can cover other obligations. In the case of assets, _________ is a means of using future purchasing power in the present before a summation has been earned. Some companies and corporations use _________ as a part of their overall corporate finance strategy.

a. Cross-collateralization
b. Credit cycle
c. Debt
d. Partial Payment

2. In mathematics, _________ are used in the study of chance and probability. They were developed to assist in the analysis of games of chance, stochastic events, and the results of scientific experiments by capturing only the mathematical properties necessary to answer probabilistic questions. Further formalizations have firmly grounded the entity in the theoretical domains of mathematics by making use of measure theory.

a. Standard deviation
b. Variance
c. Monte Carlo methods
d. Random variables

3. _________, also referred to as the discount rate, is the rate of interest which a central bank charges on the loans and advances that it extends to commercial banks and other financial intermediaries. Changes in the _________ are often used by central banks to control the money supply.

The term _________ is most commonly used by bankers to refer to the Federal Discount Rate of interest charged to Federally Chartered Savings Banks.

a. TIBOR
b. Fixed interest
c. London Interbank Offered Rate
d. Bank Rate

4. _________ proposes how rational investors will use diversification to optimize their portfolios, and how a risky asset should be priced. The basic concepts of the theory are Markowitz diversification, the efficient frontier, capital asset pricing model, the alpha and beta coefficients, the Capital Market Line and the Securities Market Line.

_________ models an asset's return as a random variable, and models a portfolio as a weighted combination of assets so that the return of a portfolio is the weighted combination of the assets' returns.

a. Consumer basket
b. Payback period
c. Market value
d. Modern portfolio theory

5. In financial and business accounting, _________ is a measure of a firm's profitability that excludes interest and income tax expenses.

EBIT = Operating Revenue - Operating Expenses (OPEX) + Non-operating Income

Operating Income = Operating Revenue - Operating Expenses

Operating income is the difference between operating revenues and operating expenses, but it is also sometimes used as a synonym for EBIT and operating profit. This is true if the firm has no non-operating income.

a. Earnings before interest and taxes
b. A Random Walk Down Wall Street
c. ABN Amro
d. AAB

6. The _________ is the weighted-average most likely outcome in gambling, probability theory, economics or finance.

In gambling and probability theory, there is usually a discrete set of possible outcomes. In this case, _________ is a measure of the relative balance of win or loss weighted by their chances of occurring.

a. A Random Walk Down Wall Street
b. ABN Amro
c. Expected Return
d. AAB

7. _________ is a concept in economics, finance, and psychology related to the behaviour of consumers and investors under uncertainty. _________ is the reluctance of a person to accept a bargain with an uncertain payoff rather than another bargain with a more certain, but possibly lower, expected payoff.

The inverse of a person's _________ is sometimes called their risk tolerance

a. Risk adjusted return on capital
b. Risk aversion
c. Discount factor
d. Risk premium

8. In statistics, _________ has two related meanings:

- the arithmetic _________
- the expected value of a random variable, which is also called the population _________.

It is sometimes stated that the '_________' is average. This is incorrect if '_________' is taken in the specific sense of 'arithmetic _________' as there are different types of averages: the _________, median, and mode. Other simple statistical analyses use measures of spread, such as range, interquartile range, or standard deviation. For a real-valued random variable X, the _________ is the expectation of X. Note that not every probability distribution has a defined _________; see the Cauchy distribution for an example.

a. Sample size
b. Mean
c. Harmonic mean
d. Probability distribution

9. In probability and statistics, the _________ of a collection of numbers is a measure of the dispersion of the numbers from their expected (mean) value. It can apply to a probability distribution, a random variable, a population or a data set. The _________ is usually denoted with the letter σ (lowercase sigma.)

a. Sample size
b. Mean
c. Kurtosis
d. Standard deviation

10. In probability theory and statistics, the _________ of a random variable, probability distribution averaging the squared distance of its possible values from the expected value (mean.) Whereas the mean is a way to describe the location of a distribution, the _________ is a way to capture its scale or degree of being spread out. The unit of _________ is the square of the unit of the original variable.

a. Semivariance
b. Monte Carlo methods
c. Harmonic mean
d. Variance

11. In probability theory and statistics, the _________ is a normalized measure of dispersion of a probability distribution. It is defined as the ratio of the standard deviation > to the mean >:

This is only defined for non-zero mean, and is most useful for variables that are always positive. It is also known as unitized risk.

a. Harmonic mean
b. Coefficient of variation
c. Random variables
d. Sample size

12. _________ is the concept of adding accumulated interest back to the principal, so that interest is earned on interest from that moment on. The act of declaring interest to be principal is called compounding (i.e., interest is compounded.) A loan, for example, may have its interest compounded every month: in this case, a loan with $100 principal and 1% interest per month would have a balance of $101 at the end of the first month.

a. 4-4-5 Calendar
b. Penny stock
c. Risk management
d. Compound interest

13. _________ is the risk that the value of an investment will decrease due to moves in market factors. The five standard _________ factors are:

- Equity risk, the risk that stock prices will change.
- Interest rate risk, the risk that interest rates will change.
- Currency risk, the risk that foreign exchange rates will change.
- Commodity risk, the risk that commodity prices (e.g. grains, metals) will change.

As with other forms of risk, _________ may be measured in a number of ways. Traditionally, this is done using a Value at Risk methodology. Value at risk is well established as a risk management technique, but it contains a number of limiting assumptions that constrain its accuracy.

a. Tracking error
b. Transaction risk
c. Currency risk
d. Market risk

14. In finance, _________ is that risk which is common to an entire market and not to any individual entity or component thereof. It should be distinguished from systemic risk which is the risk that the entire financial system will collapse as a result of some catastrophic event.

Risks can be reduced in four main ways: Avoidance, Reduction, Retention and Transfer.

a. Primary market
b. Capital surplus
c. Conglomerate merger
d. Systematic risk

15. In finance, _________ (or gearing) is borrowing money to supplement existing funds for investment in such a way that the potential positive or negative outcome is magnified and/or enhanced. It generally refers to using borrowed funds, or debt, so as to attempt to increase the returns to equity. Deleveraging is the action of reducing borrowings.

a. Pension fund
b. Financial endowment
c. Limited partnership
d. Leverage

16. _________ in finance is a risk management technique, related to hedging, that mixes a wide variety of investments within a portfolio. Because the fluctuations of a single security have less impact on a diverse portfolio, _________ minimizes the risk from any one investment.

A simple example of _________ is the following: On a particular island the entire economy consists of two companies: one that sells umbrellas and another that sells sunscreen.

a. 7-Eleven
b. 529 plan
c. Diversification
d. 4-4-5 Calendar

17. In business and finance, a _________ (also referred to as equity _________) of stock means a _________ of ownership in a corporation (company.) In the plural, stocks is often used as a synonym for _________s especially in the United States, but it is less commonly used that way outside of North America.

In the United Kingdom, South Africa, and Australia, stock can also refer to completely different financial instruments such as government bonds or, less commonly, to all kinds of marketable securities.

a. Bucket shop
b. Procter ' Gamble
c. Margin
d. Share

18. The _________, in terms of finance and investing, describes how the expected return of a stock or portfolio is correlated to the return of the financial market as a whole.

An asset with a beta of 0 means that its price is not at all correlated with the market; that asset is independent. A positive beta means that the asset generally follows the market.

a. Perpetuity
b. Current yield
c. LIBOR market model
d. Beta coefficient

19. _________ most frequently refers to the standard deviation of the continuously compounded returns of a financial instrument with a specific time horizon. It is often used to quantify the risk of the instrument over that time period. _________ is typically expressed in annualized terms, and it may either be an absolute number ($5) or a fraction of the mean (5%).

a. Volatility
b. Seasoned equity offering
c. Portfolio insurance
d. Currency swap

20. In finance, the _________ is used to determine a theoretically appropriate required rate of return of an asset, if that asset is to be added to an already well-diversified portfolio, given that asset's non-diversifiable risk. The model takes into account the asset's sensitivity to non-diversifiable risk (also known as systemic risk or market risk), often represented by the quantity beta (β) in the financial industry, as well as the expected return of the market and the expected return of a theoretical risk-free asset.

The model was introduced by Jack Treynor (1961, 1962), William Sharpe (1964), John Lintner (1965a,b) and Jan Mossin (1966) independently, building on the earlier work of Harry Markowitz on diversification and modern portfolio theory.

a. Capital asset pricing model
b. Random walk hypothesis
c. Cox-Ingersoll-Ross model
d. Hull-White model

21. The term _________ has three unrelated technical definitions, and is also used in a variety of non-technical ways.

- In financial economics, it refers to any asset used to make money, as opposed to assets used for personal enjoyment or consumption. This is an important distinction because two people can disagree sharply about the value of personal assets, one person might think a sports car is more valuable than a pickup truck, another person might have the opposite taste. But if an asset is held for the purpose of making money, taste has nothing to do with it, only differences of opinion about how much money the asset will produce. With the further assumption that people agree on the probability distribution of future cash flows, it is possible to have an objective _________ pricing model. Even without the assumption of agreement, it is possible to set rational limits on _________ value.
- In governmental accounting, it is defined as any asset used in operations with an initial useful life extending beyond one reporting period. Generally, government managers have a 'stewardship' duty to maintain _________s under their control. See International Public Sector Accounting Standards for details.
- In US tax accounting, it is defined as any property other than a list of exceptions. The main exceptions are anything held for sale, and any real estate or depreciable property used in business. Almost everything you own and use for personal purposes, pleasure or investment is a _________. If something is a _________ for tax purposes, gains or losses on sale or disposition are capital gains or capital losses. For individuals, however, capital losses on property held for personal use are generally not deductible. See the IRS publication Tax Facts about Capital Gains and Losses for details.

A well-known financial accounting textbook advises that the term be avoided except in tax accounting because it is used in so many different senses, not all of them well-defined. For example it is often used as a synonym for fixed assets or for investments in securities.

A common non-technical usage occurs when people ask that employees or the environment or something else be treated as a _________.

a. Settlement date
b. Solvency
c. Political risk
d. Capital asset

22. In business and accounting, _________s are everything of value that is owned by a person or company. The balance sheet of a firm records the monetary value of the _________s owned by the firm. The two major _________ classes are tangible _________s and intangible _________s.

a. Income
b. EBITDA
c. Asset
d. Accounts payable

23. In finance, _________ is the process of estimating the potential market value of a financial asset or liability. they can be done on assets (for example, investments in marketable securities such as stocks, options, business enterprises, or intangible assets such as patents and trademarks) or on liabilities (e.g., Bonds issued by a company.) _________s are required in many contexts including investment analysis, capital budgeting, merger and acquisition transactions, financial reporting, taxable events to determine the proper tax liability, and in litigation.

a. Procter ' Gamble
b. Margin
c. Share
d. Valuation

24. In finance, _________, also known as return on investment is the ratio of money gained or lost on an investment relative to the amount of money invested. The amount of money gained or lost may be referred to as interest, profit/loss, gain/loss, or net income/loss. The money invested may be referred to as the asset, capital, principal, or the cost basis of the investment.

a. Rate of return
b. Stock or scrip dividends
c. Doctrine of the Proper Law
d. Composiition of Creditors

25.

In finance, the _________ can be the expected rate of return above the risk-free interest rate. When measuring risk, a common sense approach is to compare the risk-free return on T-bills and the very risky return on other investments. The difference between these two returns can be interpreted as a measure of the excess return on the average risky asset. This excess return is known as the _________.

a. Risk aversion
b. Risk modeling
c. Risk adjusted return on capital
d. Risk premium

26. A _________ is a fungible, negotiable instrument representing financial value. They are broadly categorized into debt securities (such as banknotes, bonds and debentures), and equity securities; e.g., common stocks. The company or other entity issuing the _________ is called the issuer.

a. Security
b. Tracking stock
c. Book entry
d. Securities lending

27. In Modern Portfolio Theory, the _________ is the graphical representation of the Capital Asset Pricing Model. It displays the expected rate of return for an overall market as a function of systematic (non-diversifiable) risk (beta.)

The Y-Intercept (beta=0) of the _________ is equal to the risk-free interest rate.

a. Divestment
b. Certificate in Investment Performance Measurement
c. Rebalancing
d. Security market line

28. In finance, a _________ is a debt security, in which the authorized issuer owes the holders a debt and, depending on the terms of the _________, is obliged to pay interest (the coupon) and/or to repay the principal at a later date, termed maturity.

Thus a _________ is a loan: the issuer is the borrower, the _________ holder is the lender, and the coupon is the interest. _________s provide the borrower with external funds to finance long-term investments, or, in the case of government _________s, to finance current expenditure.

a. Convertible bond
b. Catastrophe bonds
c. Bond
d. Puttable bond

29. A _________ is the price of a single share of a no. of saleable stocks of the company. Once the stock is purchased, the owner becomes a shareholder of the company that issued the share.

a. Trading curb
b. Stock split
c. Whisper numbers
d. Share price

30. _________ means regulating, adapting or settling in a variety of contexts:

In commercial law, _________ means the settlement of a loss incurred on insured goods. The calculation of the amounts of compensation to be paid by or to the several interests is a complicated matter. It involves much detail and arithmetic, and requires a full and accurate knowledge of the principles of the subject.

a. Intelligent investor
b. Asset recovery
c. Adjustment
d. Equity method

1. _________ is the planning process used to determine whether a firm's long term investments such as new machinery, replacement machinery, new plants, new products, and research development projects are worth pursuing. It is budget for major capital, or investment, expenditures.

Many formal methods are used in _________, including the techniques such as

- Net present value
- Profitability index
- Internal rate of return
- Modified Internal Rate of Return
- Equivalent annuity

These methods use the incremental cash flows from each potential investment, or project. Techniques based on accounting earnings and accounting rules are sometimes used - though economists consider this to be improper - such as the accounting rate of return, and 'return on investment.' Simplified and hybrid methods are used as well, such as payback period and discounted payback period.

a. Shareholder value
b. Preferred stock
c. Financial distress
d. Capital budgeting

2. _________ in finance is a risk management technique, related to hedging, that mixes a wide variety of investments within a portfolio. Because the fluctuations of a single security have less impact on a diverse portfolio, _________ minimizes the risk from any one investment.

A simple example of _________ is the following: On a particular island the entire economy consists of two companies: one that sells umbrellas and another that sells sunscreen.

a. 7-Eleven
b. 4-4-5 Calendar
c. Diversification
d. 529 plan

3. _________ is the balance of the amounts of cash being received and paid by a business during a defined period of time, sometimes tied to a specific project. Measurement of _________ can be used

- to evaluate the state or performance of a business or project.
- to determine problems with liquidity. Being profitable does not necessarily mean being liquid. A company can fail because of a shortage of cash, even while profitable.
- to generate project rate of returns. The time of _________s into and out of projects are used as inputs to financial models such as internal rate of return, and net present value.
- to examine income or growth of a business when it is believed that accrual accounting concepts do not represent economic realities. Alternately, _________ can be used to 'validate' the net income generated by accrual accounting.

_________ as a generic term may be used differently depending on context, and certain _________ definitions may be adapted by analysts and users for their own uses. Common terms include operating _________ and free _________.

_________s can be classified into:

1. Operational _________s: Cash received or expended as a result of the company's core business activities.
2. Investment _________s: Cash received or expended through capital expenditure, investments or acquisitions.
3. Financing _________s: Cash received or expended as a result of financial activities, such as interests and dividends.

All three together - the net _________ - are necessary to reconcile the beginning cash balance to the ending cash balance. Loan draw downs or equity injections, that is just shifting of capital but no expenditure as such, are not considered in the net _________.

a. Shareholder value
b. Corporate finance
c. Cash flow
d. Real option

4. In mathematics, _________ are used in the study of chance and probability. They were developed to assist in the analysis of games of chance, stochastic events, and the results of scientific experiments by capturing only the mathematical properties necessary to answer probabilistic questions. Further formalizations have firmly grounded the entity in the theoretical domains of mathematics by making use of measure theory.

a. Variance
b. Random variables
c. Standard deviation
d. Monte Carlo methods

5. In economics, business, and accounting, a _________ is the value of money that has been used up to produce something, and hence is not available for use anymore. In business, the _________ may be one of acquisition, in which case the amount of money expended to acquire it is counted as _________. In this case, money is the input that is gone in order to acquire the thing.

a. Marginal cost
b. Fixed costs
c. Sliding scale fees
d. Cost

6. The _________ is an expected return that the provider of capital plans to earn on their investment.

Capital (money) used for funding a business should earn returns for the capital providers who risk their capital. For an investment to be worthwhile, the expected return on capital must be greater than the _________.

a. Capital intensity
b. Weighted average cost of capital
c. 4-4-5 Calendar
d. Cost of capital

7. _________ in business and economics refers to the period of time required for the return on an investment to 'repay' the sum of the original investment. For example, a $1000 investment which returned $500 per year would have a two year _________. It intuitively measures how long something takes to 'pay for itself.' _________ is widely used due to its ease of use despite recognized limitations.

a. Payback period
b. Seasoned equity offering
c. Financial Gerontology
d. Consignment stock

8. _________ or net present worth (NPW) is defined as the total present value (PV) of a time series of cash flows. It is a standard method for using the time value of money to appraise long-term projects. Used for capital budgeting, and widely throughout economics, it measures the excess or shortfall of cash flows, in present value terms, once financing charges are met.

a. Present value of costs
b. Tax shield
c. Negative gearing
d. Net present value

9. _________ is the value on a given date of a future payment or series of future payments, discounted to reflect the time value of money and other factors such as investment risk. _________ calculations are widely used in business and economics to provide a means to compare cash flows at different times on a meaningful 'like to like' basis.

The most commonly applied model of the time value of money is compound interest.

a. Present value of benefits
b. Present value
c. Net present value
d. Negative gearing

10. The _________ is a capital budgeting metric used by firms to decide whether they should make investments. It is an indicator of the efficiency or quality of an investment, as opposed to net present value (NPV), which indicates value or magnitude.

The IRR is the annualized effective compounded return rate which can be earned on the invested capital, i.e., the yield on the investment.

a. AAB
b. ABN Amro
c. A Random Walk Down Wall Street
d. Internal rate of return

11. In finance, _________, also known as return on investment is the ratio of money gained or lost on an investment relative to the amount of money invested. The amount of money gained or lost may be referred to as interest, profit/loss, gain/loss, or net income/loss. The money invested may be referred to as the asset, capital, principal, or the cost basis of the investment.

a. Composiition of Creditors
b. Doctrine of the Proper Law
c. Stock or scrip dividends
d. Rate of return

12. _________, is when a company issues common stock or shares to the public for the first time. They are often issued by smaller, younger companies seeking capital to expand, but can also be done by large privately-owned companies looking to become publicly traded.

In an _________ the issuer may obtain the assistance of an underwriting firm, which helps it determine what type of security to issue (common or preferred), best offering price and time to bring it to market.

a. Asian Financial Crisis
b. Initial public offering
c. Insolvency
d. Interest

13. An _________ is a retirement plan account that provides some tax advantages for retirement savings in the United States.

a. A Random Walk Down Wall Street
b. AAB
c. Individual Retirement Arrangement
d. ABN Amro

14. _________ identifies the relationship of investment to payoff of a proposed project. The ratio is calculated as follows:

- >

_________ is also known as Profit Investment Ratio, abbreviated to P.I. and Value Investment Ratio (V.I.R.). _________ is a good tool for ranking projects because it allows you to clearly identify the amount of value created per unit of investment, thus if you are capital constrained you wish to invest in those projects which create value most efficiently first.

a. Conditional prepayment rate
b. Profitability index
c. Capitalization rate
d. Total return

15. An _________ can be defined as a contract which provides an income stream in return for an initial payment.

An immediate _________ is an _________ for which the time between the contract date and the date of the first payment is not longer than the time interval between payments. A common use for an immediate _________ is to provide a pension to a retired person or persons.

a. Amortization
b. Intrinsic value
c. AT'T Inc.
d. Annuity

16. In finance, a _________ (non-investment grade bond, speculative grade bond or junk bond) is a bond that is rated below investment grade at the time of purchase. These bonds have a higher risk of default or other adverse credit events, but typically pay higher yields than better quality bonds in order to make them attractive to investors.

a. Private equity
b. Sharpe ratio
c. Volatility
d. High yield bond

17. The phrase _________ refers to the aspect of corporate strategy, corporate finance and management dealing with the buying, selling and combining of different companies that can aid, finance, or help a growing company in a given industry grow rapidly without having to create another business entity.

An acquisition, also known as a takeover, is the buying of one company (the 'target') by another. An acquisition may be friendly or hostile.

a. 529 plan
b. 4-4-5 Calendar
c. 7-Eleven
d. Mergers and acquisitions

18. In finance, a _________ is a debt security, in which the authorized issuer owes the holders a debt and, depending on the terms of the _________, is obliged to pay interest (the coupon) and/or to repay the principal at a later date, termed maturity.

Thus a _________ is a loan: the issuer is the borrower, the _________ holder is the lender, and the coupon is the interest. _________s provide the borrower with external funds to finance long-term investments, or, in the case of government _________s, to finance current expenditure.

a. Convertible bond
b. Puttable bond
c. Catastrophe bonds
d. Bond

19. The _________ is a financial market where participants buy and sell debt securities, usually in the form of bonds. As of 2006, the size of the international _________ is an estimated $45 trillion, of which the size of the outstanding U.S. _________ debt was $25.2 trillion.

Nearly all of the $923 billion average daily trading volume in the U.S. _________ takes place between broker-dealers and large institutions in a decentralized, over-the-counter market.

a. 4-4-5 Calendar
b. Bond market
c. 529 plan
d. Fixed income

20. _________ is a list for goods and materials held available in stock by a business. It is also used for a list of the contents of a household and for a list for testamentary purposes of the possessions of someone who has died. In accounting _________ is considered an asset.

a. Inventory
b. AAB
c. ABN Amro
d. A Random Walk Down Wall Street

1. _________ is the planning process used to determine whether a firm's long term investments such as new machinery, replacement machinery, new plants, new products, and research development projects are worth pursuing. It is budget for major capital, or investment, expenditures.

Many formal methods are used in _________, including the techniques such as

- Net present value
- Profitability index
- Internal rate of return
- Modified Internal Rate of Return
- Equivalent annuity

These methods use the incremental cash flows from each potential investment, or project. Techniques based on accounting earnings and accounting rules are sometimes used - though economists consider this to be improper - such as the accounting rate of return, and 'return on investment.' Simplified and hybrid methods are used as well, such as payback period and discounted payback period.

a. Preferred stock
b. Financial distress
c. Shareholder value
d. Capital budgeting

2. _________ is the balance of the amounts of cash being received and paid by a business during a defined period of time, sometimes tied to a specific project. Measurement of _________ can be used

- to evaluate the state or performance of a business or project.
- to determine problems with liquidity. Being profitable does not necessarily mean being liquid. A company can fail because of a shortage of cash, even while profitable.
- to generate project rate of returns. The time of _________s into and out of projects are used as inputs to financial models such as internal rate of return, and net present value.
- to examine income or growth of a business when it is believed that accrual accounting concepts do not represent economic realities. Alternately, _________ can be used to 'validate' the net income generated by accrual accounting.

_________ as a generic term may be used differently depending on context, and certain _________ definitions may be adapted by analysts and users for their own uses. Common terms include operating _________ and free _________.

_________s can be classified into:

1. Operational _________s: Cash received or expended as a result of the company's core business activities.
2. Investment _________s: Cash received or expended through capital expenditure, investments or acquisitions.
3. Financing _________s: Cash received or expended as a result of financial activities, such as interests and dividends.

All three together - the net _________ - are necessary to reconcile the beginning cash balance to the ending cash balance. Loan draw downs or equity injections, that is just shifting of capital but no expenditure as such, are not considered in the net _________.

a. Shareholder value
b. Corporate finance
c. Cash flow
d. Real option

3. In mathematics, _________ are used in the study of chance and probability. They were developed to assist in the analysis of games of chance, stochastic events, and the results of scientific experiments by capturing only the mathematical properties necessary to answer probabilistic questions. Further formalizations have firmly grounded the entity in the theoretical domains of mathematics by making use of measure theory.

a. Random variables
b. Standard deviation
c. Monte Carlo methods
d. Variance

4. In business and accounting, _________s are everything of value that is owned by a person or company. The balance sheet of a firm records the monetary value of the _________s owned by the firm. The two major _________ classes are tangible _________s and intangible _________s.

a. Accounts payable
b. Income
c. EBITDA
d. Asset

5. In economics, business, and accounting, a _________ is the value of money that has been used up to produce something, and hence is not available for use anymore. In business, the _________ may be one of acquisition, in which case the amount of money expended to acquire it is counted as _________. In this case, money is the input that is gone in order to acquire the thing.

a. Sliding scale fees
b. Cost
c. Marginal cost
d. Fixed costs

6. _________, _________ includes the direct costs attributable to the production of the goods sold by a company. This amount includes the materials cost used in creating the goods along with the direct labor costs used to produce the good. It excludes indirect expenses such as distribution costs and sales force costs.

a. Goodwill
b. Net profit
c. Cost of goods sold
d. Deferred financing costs

7. _________ is a term used in accounting, economics and finance to spread the cost of an asset over the span of several years.

In simple words we can say that _________ is the reduction in the value of an asset due to usage, passage of time, wear and tear, technological outdating or obsolescence, depletion or other such factors.

In accounting, _________ is a term used to describe any method of attributing the historical or purchase cost of an asset across its useful life, roughly corresponding to normal wear and tear.

a. Matching principle
b. Depreciation
c. Deferred financing costs
d. Bottom line

8. In business, _________ is income that a company receives from its normal business activities, usually from the sale of goods and services to customers. Some companies also receive _________ from interest, dividends or royalties paid to them by other companies. _________ may refer to business income in general, or it may refer to the amount, in a monetary unit, received during a period of time, as in 'Last year, Company X had _________ of $32 million.'

In many countries, including the UK, _________ is referred to as turnover.

a. Bottom line
b. Furniture, Fixtures and Equipment
c. Matching principle
d. Revenue

9. An _________ can be defined as a contract which provides an income stream in return for an initial payment.

An immediate _________ is an _________ for which the time between the contract date and the date of the first payment is not longer than the time interval between payments. A common use for an immediate _________ is to provide a pension to a retired person or persons.

a. Amortization
b. AT'T Inc.
c. Annuity
d. Intrinsic value

10. The _________, effective annual interest rate, Annual Equivalent Rate (AER) or simply effective rate is the interest rate on a loan or financial product restated from the nominal interest rate as an interest rate with annual compound interest. It is used to compare the annual interest between loans with different compounding terms (daily, monthly, annually, or other.)

The _________ differs in two important respects from the annual percentage rate (APR):

1. the _________ generally does not incorporate one-time charges such as front-end fees;
2. the _________ is (generally) not defined by legal or regulatory authorities (as APR is in many jurisdictions.)

By contrast, the 'effective APR' is used as a legal term, where front-fees and other costs can be included, as defined by local law.

Annual Percentage Yield or effective annual yield is the analogous concept used for savings or investment products, such as a certificate of deposit.

a. Effective interest rate
b. ABN Amro
c. AAB
d. A Random Walk Down Wall Street

11. _________ or economic opportunity loss is the value of the next best alternative foregone as the result of making a decision. _________ analysis is an important part of a company's decision-making processes but is not treated as an actual cost in any financial statement. The next best thing that a person can engage in is referred to as the _________ of doing the best thing and ignoring the next best thing to be done.

a. A Random Walk Down Wall Street
b. AAB
c. ABN Amro
d. Opportunity cost

12. In economics and business decision-making, _________ are costs that cannot be recovered once they have been incurred. _________ are sometimes contrasted with variable costs, which are the costs that will change due to the proposed course of action, and prospective costs which are costs that will be incurred if an action is taken. In microeconomic theory, only variable costs are relevant to a decision.

a. Hindsight bias
b. Hyperbolic discounting
c. 4-4-5 Calendar
d. Sunk costs

13. _________ or financing is to provide capital (funds), which means money for a project, a person, a business or any other private or public institutions.

Those funds can be allocated for either short term or long term purposes. The health fund is a new way of _________ private healthcare centers.

a. Product life cycle
b. Synthetic CDO
c. Proxy fight
d. Funding

14. _________ is a financial metric which represents operating liquidity available to a business. Along with fixed assets such as plant and equipment, _________ is considered a part of operating capital. It is calculated as current assets minus current liabilities.

a. 529 plan
b. 4-4-5 Calendar
c. Working capital management
d. Working capital

15. In finance, the _________ (continuing value or horizon value) of a security is the present value at a future point in time of all future cash flows when we expect stable growth rate forever. It is most often used in multi-stage discounted cash flow analysis, and allows for the limitation of cash flow projections to a several-year period. Forecasting results beyond such a period is impractical and exposes such projections to a variety of risks limiting their validity, primarily the great uncertainty involved in predicting industry and macroeconomic conditions beyond a few years.

a. Negative gearing
b. Refinancing risk
c. Terminal value
d. Discounted cash flow

16. The _________ is the current method of accelerated asset depreciation required by the United States income tax code. Under _________, all assets are divided into classes which dictate the number of years over which an asset's cost will be recovered.

Prior to the Accelerated Cost Recovery System (ACRS), most capital purchases were depreciated using a straight line technique, that allowed for the depreciation of the asset over its useful life.

a. 7-Eleven
b. Modified Accelerated Cost Recovery System
c. 4-4-5 Calendar
d. 529 plan

17. _________ is a legally declared inability or impairment of ability of an individual or organization to pay their creditors. Creditors may file a _________ petition against a debtor ('involuntary _________') in an effort to recoup a portion of what they are owed or initiate a restructuring. In the majority of cases, however, _________ is initiated by the debtor (a 'voluntary _________' that is filed by the bankrupt individual or organization.)

a. Debt settlement
b. 4-4-5 Calendar
c. 529 plan
d. Bankruptcy

1. _________ is the planning process used to determine whether a firm's long term investments such as new machinery, replacement machinery, new plants, new products, and research development projects are worth pursuing. It is budget for major capital, or investment, expenditures.

Many formal methods are used in _________, including the techniques such as

- Net present value
- Profitability index
- Internal rate of return
- Modified Internal Rate of Return
- Equivalent annuity

These methods use the incremental cash flows from each potential investment, or project. Techniques based on accounting earnings and accounting rules are sometimes used - though economists consider this to be improper - such as the accounting rate of return, and 'return on investment.' Simplified and hybrid methods are used as well, such as payback period and discounted payback period.

a. Preferred stock
b. Shareholder value
c. Capital budgeting
d. Financial distress

2. In mathematics, _________ are used in the study of chance and probability. They were developed to assist in the analysis of games of chance, stochastic events, and the results of scientific experiments by capturing only the mathematical properties necessary to answer probabilistic questions. Further formalizations have firmly grounded the entity in the theoretical domains of mathematics by making use of measure theory.

a. Monte Carlo methods
b. Variance
c. Standard deviation
d. Random variables

3. In corporate finance, _________ analysis applies put option and call option valuation techniques to capital budgeting decisions. A _________ itself, is the right--but not the obligation--to undertake some business decision; typically the option to make, or abandon, a capital investment. For example, the opportunity to invest in the expansion of a firm's factory, or alternatively to sell the factory, is a _________.

a. Real option
b. Cash flow
c. Book building
d. Capital budgeting

4. _________ is the balance of the amounts of cash being received and paid by a business during a defined period of time, sometimes tied to a specific project. Measurement of _________ can be used

- to evaluate the state or performance of a business or project.
- to determine problems with liquidity. Being profitable does not necessarily mean being liquid. A company can fail because of a shortage of cash, even while profitable.
- to generate project rate of returns. The time of _________s into and out of projects are used as inputs to financial models such as internal rate of return, and net present value.
- to examine income or growth of a business when it is believed that accrual accounting concepts do not represent economic realities. Alternately, _________ can be used to 'validate' the net income generated by accrual accounting.

_________ as a generic term may be used differently depending on context, and certain _________ definitions may be adapted by analysts and users for their own uses. Common terms include operating _________ and free _________.

_________s can be classified into:

1. Operational _________s: Cash received or expended as a result of the company's core business activities.
2. Investment _________s: Cash received or expended through capital expenditure, investments or acquisitions.
3. Financing _________s: Cash received or expended as a result of financial activities, such as interests and dividends.

All three together - the net _________ - are necessary to reconcile the beginning cash balance to the ending cash balance. Loan draw downs or equity injections, that is just shifting of capital but no expenditure as such, are not considered in the net _________.

a. Corporate finance
b. Shareholder value
c. Real option
d. Cash flow

5. An _________ is a contract written by a seller that conveys to the buyer the right -- but not the obligation -- to buy (in the case of a call _________) or to sell (in the case of a put _________) a particular asset, such as a piece of property such as, among others, a futures contract. In return for granting the _________, the seller collects a payment (the premium) from the buyer.

For example, buying a call _________ provides the right to buy a specified quantity of a security at a set strike price at some time on or before expiration, while buying a put _________ provides the right to sell.

a. Amortization
b. Option
c. Annuity
d. AT'T Mobility LLC

6. _________ is a concept in economics, finance, and psychology related to the behaviour of consumers and investors under uncertainty. _________ is the reluctance of a person to accept a bargain with an uncertain payoff rather than another bargain with a more certain, but possibly lower, expected payoff.

The inverse of a person's _________ is sometimes called their risk tolerance

a. Discount factor
b. Risk premium
c. Risk adjusted return on capital
d. Risk aversion

7. _________ is a process of analyzing possible future events by considering alternative possible outcomes (scenarios.) The analysis is designed to allow improved decision-making by allowing consideration of outcomes and their implications.

For example, in economics and finance, a financial institution might attempt to forecast several possible scenarios for the economy (e.g. rapid growth, moderate growth, slow growth) and it might also attempt to forecast financial market returns (for bonds, stocks and cash) in each of those scenarios.

a. Detection Risk
b. Scenario analysis
c. 529 plan
d. 4-4-5 Calendar

8. _________ are a class of computational algorithms that rely on repeated random sampling to compute their results. _________ are often used when simulating physical and mathematical systems. Because of their reliance on repeated computation and random or pseudo-random numbers, _________ are most suited to calculation by a computer.

_________ in finance are often used to calculate the value of companies, to evaluate investments in projects at corporate level or to evaluate financial derivatives. The method is intended for financial analysts who want to construct stochastic or probabilistic financial models as opposed to the traditional static and deterministic models.

a. Semivariance
b. Sample size
c. Monte Carlo methods
d. Correlation

9. _________ is the study of how the variation (uncertainty) in the output of a mathematical model can be apportioned, qualitatively or quantitatively, to different sources of variation in the input of a model .

In more general terms uncertainty and sensitivity analyses investigate the robustness of a study when the study includes some form of mathematical modelling. While uncertainty analysis studies the overall uncertainty in the conclusions of the study, _________ tries to identify what source of uncertainty weights more on the study's conclusions.

a. Sensitivity analysis
b. Proxy fight
c. Synthetic CDO
d. Golden parachute

10. A _________ is a decision support tool that uses a tree-like graph or model of decisions and their possible consequences, including chance event outcomes, resource costs, and utility. _________s are commonly used in operations research, specifically in decision analysis, to help identify a strategy most likely to reach a goal. Another use of _________s is as a descriptive means for calculating conditional probabilities.

a. 7-Eleven
b. 4-4-5 Calendar
c. Decision tree
d. 529 plan

11. In probability theory and statistics, a _________ identifies either the probability of each value of an unidentified random variable (when the variable is discrete), or the probability of the value falling within a particular interval (when the variable is continuous.) The _________ describes the range of possible values that a random variable can attain and the probability that the value of the random variable is within any (measurable) subset of that range. The Normal distribution, often called the 'bell curve'

When the random variable takes values in the set of real numbers, the _________ is completely described by the cumulative distribution function, whose value at each real x is the probability that the random variable is smaller than or equal to x.

a. Correlation
b. Probability distribution
c. P-value
d. Standard deviation

12. _________ is the probability of some event A, given the occurrence of some other event B. _________ is written P(A | B), and is read 'the probability of A, given B'.

Joint probability is the probability of two events in conjunction. That is, it is the probability of both events together.

a. 7-Eleven
b. 529 plan
c. Conditional probability
d. 4-4-5 Calendar

13. In finance, _________, also known as return on investment is the ratio of money gained or lost on an investment relative to the amount of money invested. The amount of money gained or lost may be referred to as interest, profit/loss, gain/loss, or net income/loss. The money invested may be referred to as the asset, capital, principal, or the cost basis of the investment.

a. Composiition of Creditors
b. Rate of return
c. Stock or scrip dividends
d. Doctrine of the Proper Law

14. _________ in finance is a risk management technique, related to hedging, that mixes a wide variety of investments within a portfolio. Because the fluctuations of a single security have less impact on a diverse portfolio, _________ minimizes the risk from any one investment.

A simple example of _________ is the following: On a particular island the entire economy consists of two companies: one that sells umbrellas and another that sells sunscreen.

a. 529 plan
b. 4-4-5 Calendar
c. 7-Eleven
d. Diversification

15. _________ is a fee paid on borrowed assets. It is the price paid for the use of borrowed money , or, money earned by deposited funds . Assets that are sometimes lent with _________ include money, shares, consumer goods through hire purchase, major assets such as aircraft, and even entire factories in finance lease arrangements.

a. A Random Walk Down Wall Street
b. Insolvency
c. AAB
d. Interest

16. An _________ is the price a borrower pays for the use of money they do not own, and the return a lender receives for deferring the use of funds, by lending it to the borrower. _________s are normally expressed as a percentage rate over the period of one year.

_________s targets are also a vital tool of monetary policy and are used to control variables like investment, inflation, and unemployment.

a. AAB
b. Interest rate
c. ABN Amro
d. A Random Walk Down Wall Street

17. In finance, the _________ is used to determine a theoretically appropriate required rate of return of an asset, if that asset is to be added to an already well-diversified portfolio, given that asset's non-diversifiable risk. The model takes into account the asset's sensitivity to non-diversifiable risk (also known as systemic risk or market risk), often represented by the quantity beta (β) in the financial industry, as well as the expected return of the market and the expected return of a theoretical risk-free asset.

The model was introduced by Jack Treynor (1961, 1962), William Sharpe (1964), John Lintner (1965a,b) and Jan Mossin (1966) independently, building on the earlier work of Harry Markowitz on diversification and modern portfolio theory.

a. Random walk hypothesis
b. Hull-White model
c. Capital asset pricing model
d. Cox-Ingersoll-Ross model

18. In e-business terms, a _________ is an organization that originated and does business purely through the internet, they have no physical store (brick and mortar) where customers can shop. Examples of large _________ companies include Amazon.com and Netflix.com. There are also many smaller, niche oriented _________ mail order companies such as women's travel accessories company Christine Columbus and fashion jewelry merchant Jewels of Denial.

a. 529 plan
b. The Dogs of the Dow
c. 4-4-5 Calendar
d. Pure play

19. The role of the _________ is to issue accounting standards in the United Kingdom. It is recognised for that purpose under the Companies Act 1985. It took over the task of setting accounting standards from the Accounting Standards Committee (ASC) in 1990.

a. A Random Walk Down Wall Street
b. AAB
c. ABN Amro
d. Accounting Standards Board

20. _________ is the field of accountancy concerned with the preparation of financial statements for decision makers, such as stockholders, suppliers, banks, employees, government agencies, owners, and other stakeholders. The fundamental need for _________ is to reduce principal-agent problem by measuring and monitoring agents' performance and reporting the results to interested users.

_________ is used to prepare accounting information for people outside the organization or not involved in the day to day running of the company.

a. 7-Eleven
b. 529 plan
c. 4-4-5 Calendar
d. Financial Accounting

21. The _________ is a private, not-for-profit organization whose primary purpose is to develop generally accepted accounting principles (GAAP) within the United States in the public's interest. The Securities and Exchange Commission (SEC) designated the _________ as the organization responsible for setting accounting standards for public companies in the U.S. It was created in 1973, replacing the Accounting Principles Board and the Committee on Accounting Procedure of the American Institute of Certified Public Accountants. The _________'s mission is 'to establish and improve standards of financial accounting and reporting for the guidance and education of the public, including issuers, auditors, and users of financial information.'

The _________ is not a governmental body.

a. Federal Deposit Insurance Corporation
b. Financial Accounting Standards Board
c. KPMG
d. World Congress of Accountants

1. In economics, business, and accounting, a _________ is the value of money that has been used up to produce something, and hence is not available for use anymore. In business, the _________ may be one of acquisition, in which case the amount of money expended to acquire it is counted as _________. In this case, money is the input that is gone in order to acquire the thing.

a. Fixed costs
b. Sliding scale fees
c. Marginal cost
d. Cost

2. The _________ is an expected return that the provider of capital plans to earn on their investment.

Capital (money) used for funding a business should earn returns for the capital providers who risk their capital. For an investment to be worthwhile, the expected return on capital must be greater than the _________.

a. Capital intensity
b. 4-4-5 Calendar
c. Weighted average cost of capital
d. Cost of capital

3. In finance, _________ refers to the way a corporation finances its assets through some combination of equity, debt, or hybrid securities. A firm's _________ is then the composition or 'structure' of its liabilities. For example, a firm that sells $20 billion in equity and $80 billion in debt is said to be 20% equity-financed and 80% debt-financed.

a. Rights issue
b. Market for corporate control
c. Book building
d. Capital structure

4. In mathematics, _________ are used in the study of chance and probability. They were developed to assist in the analysis of games of chance, stochastic events, and the results of scientific experiments by capturing only the mathematical properties necessary to answer probabilistic questions. Further formalizations have firmly grounded the entity in the theoretical domains of mathematics by making use of measure theory.

a. Monte Carlo methods
b. Standard deviation
c. Variance
d. Random variables

5. _________ is the price at which an asset would trade in a competitive Walrasian auction setting. _________ is often used interchangeably with open _________, fair value or fair _________, although these terms have distinct definitions in different standards, and may differ in some circumstances.

International Valuation Standards defines _________ as 'the estimated amount for which a property should exchange on the date of valuation between a willing buyer and a willing seller in an arm'e;s-length transaction after proper marketing wherein the parties had each acted knowledgeably, prudently, and without compulsion.'

_________ is a concept distinct from market price, which is 'e;the price at which one can transact'e;, while _________ is 'e;the true underlying value'e; according to theoretical standards.

a. Debt restructuring
b. T-Model
c. Wrap account
d. Market value

6. In accounting, _________ or *Carrying value* is the value of an asset according to its balance sheet account balance. For assets, the value is based on the original cost of the asset less any depreciation, amortization or impairment costs made against the asset. A company's _________ is its total assets minus intangible assets and liabilities.

a. Book value
b. Current liabilities
c. Pro forma
d. Retained earnings

7. The _________ is the rate that a company is expected to pay to finance its assets. WACC is the minimum return that a company must earn on existing asset base to satisfy its creditors, owners, and other providers of capital.

Companies raise money from a number of sources: common equity, preferred equity, straight debt, convertible debt, exchangeable debt, warrants, options, pension liabilities, executive stock options, governmental subsidies, and so on.

a. 4-4-5 Calendar
b. Weighted average cost of capital
c. Cost of capital
d. Capital intensity

8. _________ means regulating, adapting or settling in a variety of contexts:

In commercial law, _________ means the settlement of a loss incurred on insured goods. The calculation of the amounts of compensation to be paid by or to the several interests is a complicated matter. It involves much detail and arithmetic, and requires a full and accurate knowledge of the principles of the subject.

a. Asset recovery
b. Intelligent investor
c. Equity method
d. Adjustment

9. In economics, a _________ is a mechanism that allows people to easily buy and sell (trade) financial securities (such as stocks and bonds), commodities (such as precious metals or agricultural goods), and other fungible items of value at low transaction costs and at prices that reflect the efficient-market hypothesis.

_________s have evolved significantly over several hundred years and are undergoing constant innovation to improve liquidity.

Both general markets (where many commodities are traded) and specialized markets (where only one commodity is traded) exist.

a. Financial market
b. Delta hedging
c. Cost of carry
d. Secondary market

10. _________, is when a company issues common stock or shares to the public for the first time. They are often issued by smaller, younger companies seeking capital to expand, but can also be done by large privately-owned companies looking to become publicly traded.

In an _________ the issuer may obtain the assistance of an underwriting firm, which helps it determine what type of security to issue (common or preferred), best offering price and time to bring it to market.

a. Interest
b. Asian Financial Crisis
c. Insolvency
d. Initial public offering

11. _________ is that which is owed; usually referencing assets owed, but the term can cover other obligations. In the case of assets, _________ is a means of using future purchasing power in the present before a summation has been earned. Some companies and corporations use _________ as a part of their overall corporate finance strategy.

a. Debt
b. Cross-collateralization
c. Credit cycle
d. Partial Payment

12. _________ or financing is to provide capital (funds), which means money for a project, a person, a business or any other private or public institutions.

Those funds can be allocated for either short term or long term purposes. The health fund is a new way of _________ private healthcare centers.

a. Product life cycle
b. Funding
c. Proxy fight
d. Synthetic CDO

13. _________ is typically a higher ranking stock than voting shares, and its terms are negotiated between the corporation and the investor.

_________ usually carry no voting rights, but may carry superior priority over common stock in the payment of dividends and upon liquidation. _________ may carry a dividend that is paid out prior to any dividends to common stock holders.

a. Follow-on offering
b. Trade-off theory
c. Preferred stock
d. Second lien loan

14. In accounting, _________ refers to the portion of net income which is retained by the corporation rather than distributed to its owners as dividends. Similarly, if the corporation makes a loss, then that loss is retained and called variously retained losses, accumulated losses or accumulated deficit. _________ and losses are cumulative from year to year with losses offsetting earnings.

a. Matching principle
b. Historical cost
c. Generally Accepted Accounting Principles
d. Retained earnings

15. In finance, the _________ is used to determine a theoretically appropriate required rate of return of an asset, if that asset is to be added to an already well-diversified portfolio, given that asset's non-diversifiable risk. The model takes into account the asset's sensitivity to non-diversifiable risk (also known as systemic risk or market risk), often represented by the quantity beta (β) in the financial industry, as well as the expected return of the market and the expected return of a theoretical risk-free asset.

The model was introduced by Jack Treynor (1961, 1962), William Sharpe (1964), John Lintner (1965a,b) and Jan Mossin (1966) independently, building on the earlier work of Harry Markowitz on diversification and modern portfolio theory.

a. Random walk hypothesis
b. Cox-Ingersoll-Ross model
c. Hull-White model
d. Capital asset pricing model

16. In finance, _________, also known as return on investment is the ratio of money gained or lost on an investment relative to the amount of money invested. The amount of money gained or lost may be referred to as interest, profit/loss, gain/loss, or net income/loss. The money invested may be referred to as the asset, capital, principal, or the cost basis of the investment.

a. Composiition of Creditors
b. Doctrine of the Proper Law
c. Stock or scrip dividends
d. Rate of return

17. A _________ is a payment made by a corporation to its shareholder members. When a corporation earns a profit or surplus, that money can be put to two uses: it can either be re-invested in the business (called retained earnings), or it can be paid to the shareholders as a _________. Many corporations retain a portion of their earnings and pay the remainder as a _________.

a. Dividend
b. Special dividend
c. Dividend puzzle
d. Dividend yield

18. In financial and business accounting, _________ is a measure of a firm's profitability that excludes interest and income tax expenses.

EBIT = Operating Revenue - Operating Expenses (OPEX) + Non-operating Income

Operating Income = Operating Revenue - Operating Expenses

Operating income is the difference between operating revenues and operating expenses, but it is also sometimes used as a synonym for EBIT and operating profit. This is true if the firm has no non-operating income.

a. AAB
b. A Random Walk Down Wall Street
c. ABN Amro
d. Earnings before interest and taxes

19. _________ is a variant of the Discounted cash flow model, a method for valuing a stock or business. Often used to provide difficult-to-resolve valuation issues for litigation, tax planning, and business transactions that are currently off market.

It assumes that the company issues a dividend that has a current value of D that grows at a constant rate g. It also assumes that the required rate of return for the stock remains constant at k which is equal to the cost of equity for that company. It involves summing the infinite series which gives the value of price current P.

a. Gordon growth model
b. Stock or scrip dividends
c. Special journals
d. Securitization

20.

In finance, the _________ can be the expected rate of return above the risk-free interest rate. When measuring risk, a common sense approach is to compare the risk-free return on T-bills and the very risky return on other investments. The difference between these two returns can be interpreted as a measure of the excess return on the average risky asset. This excess return is known as the _________.

a. Risk adjusted return on capital
b. Risk premium
c. Risk modeling
d. Risk aversion

21. _________ is a form of corporation equity ownership represented in the securities. It is dangerous in comparison to preferred shares and some other investment options, in that in the event of bankruptcy, _________ investors receive their funds after preferred stockholders, bondholders, creditors, etc. On the other hand, common shares on average perform better than preferred shares or bonds over time.

a. Stock market bubble
b. Stop-limit order
c. Stock split
d. Common stock

22. In economics and finance, _________ is the change in total cost that arises when the quantity produced changes by one unit. It is the cost of producing one more unit of a good. Mathematically, the _________ function is expressed as the first derivative of the total cost (TC) function with respect to quantity (Q). Note that the _________ may change with volume, and so at each level of production, the _________ is the cost of the next unit produced.

A typical _________ Curve

>

a. Sliding scale fees
b. Fixed costs
c. Cost accounting
d. Marginal cost

23. _________ are costs incurred on the purchase of land, buildings, construction and equipment to be used in the production of goods or the rendering of services. In other words, the total cost needed to bring a project to a commercially operable status. However, _________ are not limited to the initial construction of a factory or other business.

a. Capital costs
b. Trade-off
c. Defined contribution plan
d. Capital outflow

24. _________ in finance is a risk management technique, related to hedging, that mixes a wide variety of investments within a portfolio. Because the fluctuations of a single security have less impact on a diverse portfolio, _________ minimizes the risk from any one investment.

A simple example of _________ is the following: On a particular island the entire economy consists of two companies: one that sells umbrellas and another that sells sunscreen.

a. 4-4-5 Calendar
b. 529 plan
c. 7-Eleven
d. Diversification

25. _________ refers to the additional value of a commodity over the cost of commodities used to produce it from the previous stage of production. An example is the price of gasoline at the pump over the price of the oil in it. In national accounts used in macroeconomics, it refers to the contribution of the factors of production, i.e., land, labor, and capital goods, to raising the value of a product and corresponds to the incomes received by the owners of these factors.

a. Value added
b. Deregulation
c. Supply shock
d. Demand shock

1. In finance, _________ refers to the way a corporation finances its assets through some combination of equity, debt, or hybrid securities. A firm's _________ is then the composition or 'structure' of its liabilities. For example, a firm that sells $20 billion in equity and $80 billion in debt is said to be 20% equity-financed and 80% debt-financed.

a. Market for corporate control
b. Rights issue
c. Book building
d. Capital structure

2. In finance, _________ (or gearing) is borrowing money to supplement existing funds for investment in such a way that the potential positive or negative outcome is magnified and/or enhanced. It generally refers to using borrowed funds, or debt, so as to attempt to increase the returns to equity. Deleveraging is the action of reducing borrowings.

a. Leverage
b. Financial endowment
c. Pension fund
d. Limited partnership

3. _________ is the corporate management term for the act of reorganizing the legal, ownership, operational, or other structures of a company for the purpose of making it more profitable or better organized for its present needs. Alternate reasons for restructing include a change of ownership or ownership structure, demerger repositioning debt _________ and financial _________.

a. Concentrated stock
b. Restructuring
c. Cross-border leasing
d. Day trading

4. _________ is normally any risk associated with any form of financing.

Depending on the nature of the investment, the type of 'investment' risk will vary. High risk investments have greater potential rewards, but you may lose your money instead by taking the risk for more money.

a. Liquidating dividend
b. Revaluation
c. Stock market index option
d. Financial risk

5. In economics, business, and accounting, a _________ is the value of money that has been used up to produce something, and hence is not available for use anymore. In business, the _________ may be one of acquisition, in which case the amount of money expended to acquire it is counted as _________. In this case, money is the input that is gone in order to acquire the thing.

a. Sliding scale fees
b. Marginal cost
c. Fixed costs
d. Cost

6. _________ are costs incurred on the purchase of land, buildings, construction and equipment to be used in the production of goods or the rendering of services. In other words, the total cost needed to bring a project to a commercially operable status. However, _________ are not limited to the initial construction of a factory or other business.

a. Trade-off
b. Capital outflow
c. Defined contribution plan
d. Capital costs

7. _________ has many definitions and is not easily analysed. In general, it represents the capital investment necessary for a business to function. Consequently, it is not a measure of assets, but of capital investment: stock or shares and long-term liabilities.

a. PEG ratio
b. Return on assets
c. Times interest earned
d. Capital employed

8. _________ is that which is owed; usually referencing assets owed, but the term can cover other obligations. In the case of assets, _________ is a means of using future purchasing power in the present before a summation has been earned. Some companies and corporations use _________ as a part of their overall corporate finance strategy.

a. Debt
b. Partial Payment
c. Credit cycle
d. Cross-collateralization

9. In mathematics, _________ are used in the study of chance and probability. They were developed to assist in the analysis of games of chance, stochastic events, and the results of scientific experiments by capturing only the mathematical properties necessary to answer probabilistic questions. Further formalizations have firmly grounded the entity in the theoretical domains of mathematics by making use of measure theory.

a. Monte Carlo methods
b. Standard deviation
c. Variance
d. Random variables

10. A _________ is the price of a single share of a no. of saleable stocks of the company. Once the stock is purchased, the owner becomes a shareholder of the company that issued the share.

a. Trading curb
b. Whisper numbers
c. Stock split
d. Share price

11. In accounting, _________ or *Carrying value* is the value of an asset according to its balance sheet account balance. For assets, the value is based on the original cost of the asset less any depreciation, amortization or impairment costs made against the asset. A company's _________ is its total assets minus intangible assets and liabilities.

a. Pro forma
b. Retained earnings
c. Current liabilities
d. Book value

12. In business and finance, a _________ (also referred to as equity _________) of stock means a _________ of ownership in a corporation (company.) In the plural, stocks is often used as a synonym for _________s especially in the United States, but it is less commonly used that way outside of North America.

In the United Kingdom, South Africa, and Australia, stock can also refer to completely different financial instruments such as government bonds or, less commonly, to all kinds of marketable securities.

a. Bucket shop
b. Procter ' Gamble
c. Share
d. Margin

13. The _________ is a measure of how revenue growth translates into growth in operating income. It is a measure of leverage, and of how risky (volatile) a company's operating income is.

There are various measures of _________, which can be interpreted analogously to financial leverage.

a. Average accounting return
b. Asset turnover
c. Invested capital
d. Operating leverage

14. _________ are business expenses that are not dependent on the level of production or sales. They tend to be time-related, such as salaries or rents being paid per month. This is in contrast to Variable costs, which are volume-related (and are paid per quantity.)

a. Sliding scale fees
b. Marginal cost
c. Transaction cost
d. Fixed costs

15. _________ are expenses that change in proportion to the activity of a business. In other words, _________ are the sum of marginal costs. It can also be considered normal costs. Along with fixed costs, _________ make up the two components of total cost. Direct Costs, however, are costs that can be associated with a particular cost object.

a. Variable costs
b. Cost accounting
c. Fixed costs
d. Transaction cost

16. In cost-volume-profit analysis, a form of management accounting, _________ is the marginal profit per unit sale. It is a useful quantity in carrying out various calculations, and can be used as a measure of operating leverage.

The Total _________ is Total Revenue (TR, or Sales) minus Total Variable Cost (TVC):

TContribution margin = TR >– TVC

The Unit _________ (C) is Unit Revenue (Price, P) minus Unit Variable Cost (V):

C = P >– V

The _________ Ratio is the percentage of Contribution over Total Revenue, which can be calculated from the unit contribution over unit price or total contribution over Total Revenue:

>

For instance, if the price is $10 and the unit variable cost is $2, then the unit _________ is $8, and the _________ ratio is $8/ $10 = 80%.

a. Contribution margin
b. 4-4-5 Calendar
c. 7-Eleven
d. 529 plan

17. In finance, a _________ is collateral that the holder of a position in securities, options, or futures contracts has to deposit to cover the credit risk of his counterparty (most often his broker.) This risk can arise if the holder has done any of the following:

- borrowed cash from the counterparty to buy securities or options,
- sold securities or options short, or
- entered into a futures contract.

The collateral can be in the form of cash or securities, and it is deposited in a _________ account. On U.S. futures exchanges, '_________' was formally called performance bond.

_________ buying is buying securities with cash borrowed from a broker, using other securities as collateral.

a. Credit
b. Procter ' Gamble
c. Margin
d. Share

18. In financial and business accounting, _________ is a measure of a firm's profitability that excludes interest and income tax expenses.

EBIT = Operating Revenue - Operating Expenses (OPEX) + Non-operating Income

Operating Income = Operating Revenue - Operating Expenses

Operating income is the difference between operating revenues and operating expenses, but it is also sometimes used as a synonym for EBIT and operating profit. This is true if the firm has no non-operating income.

a. A Random Walk Down Wall Street
b. Earnings before interest and taxes
c. AAB
d. ABN Amro

19. _________ is a fee paid on borrowed assets. It is the price paid for the use of borrowed money , or, money earned by deposited funds . Assets that are sometimes lent with _________ include money, shares, consumer goods through hire purchase, major assets such as aircraft, and even entire factories in finance lease arrangements.

a. A Random Walk Down Wall Street
b. AAB
c. Interest
d. Insolvency

20. _________ is the concept of adding accumulated interest back to the principal, so that interest is earned on interest from that moment on. The act of declaring interest to be principal is called compounding (i.e., interest is compounded.) A loan, for example, may have its interest compounded every month: in this case, a loan with $100 principal and 1% interest per month would have a balance of $101 at the end of the first month.

a. 4-4-5 Calendar
b. Penny stock
c. Risk management
d. Compound interest

21. _________ is the balance of the amounts of cash being received and paid by a business during a defined period of time, sometimes tied to a specific project. Measurement of _________ can be used

- to evaluate the state or performance of a business or project.
- to determine problems with liquidity. Being profitable does not necessarily mean being liquid. A company can fail because of a shortage of cash, even while profitable.
- to generate project rate of returns. The time of _________s into and out of projects are used as inputs to financial models such as internal rate of return, and net present value.
- to examine income or growth of a business when it is believed that accrual accounting concepts do not represent economic realities. Alternately, _________ can be used to 'validate' the net income generated by accrual accounting.

_________ as a generic term may be used differently depending on context, and certain _________ definitions may be adapted by analysts and users for their own uses. Common terms include operating _________ and free _________.

_________s can be classified into:

1. Operational _________s: Cash received or expended as a result of the company's core business activities.
2. Investment _________s: Cash received or expended through capital expenditure, investments or acquisitions.
3. Financing _________s: Cash received or expended as a result of financial activities, such as interests and dividends.

All three together - the net _________ - are necessary to reconcile the beginning cash balance to the ending cash balance. Loan draw downs or equity injections, that is just shifting of capital but no expenditure as such, are not considered in the net _________.

a. Corporate finance
b. Shareholder value
c. Real option
d. Cash flow

22. _________, refers to consumption opportunity gained by an entity within a specified time frame, which is generally expressed in monetary terms. However, for households and individuals, '_________ is the sum of all the wages, salaries, profits, interests payments, rents and other forms of earnings received... in a given period of time.' For firms, _________ generally refers to net-profit: what remains of revenue after expenses have been subtracted.

a. Income
b. Accrual
c. OIBDA
d. Annual report

23. _________ is the difference between operating revenues and operating expenses, but it is also sometimes used as a synonym for EBIT and operating profit. This is true if the firm has no non-_________.

A professional investor contemplating a change to the capital structure of a firm (e.g., through a leveraged buyout) first evaluates a firm's fundamental earnings potential (reflected by Earnings Before Interest, Taxes, Depreciation and Amortization EBITDA and EBIT), and then determines the optimal use of debt vs. equity.

a. ABN Amro
b. AAB
c. Operating income
d. A Random Walk Down Wall Street

24. _________ or financing is to provide capital (funds), which means money for a project, a person, a business or any other private or public institutions.

Those funds can be allocated for either short term or long term purposes. The health fund is a new way of _________ private healthcare centers.

a. Product life cycle
b. Funding
c. Proxy fight
d. Synthetic CDO

25. _________ is a legally declared inability or impairment of ability of an individual or organization to pay their creditors. Creditors may file a _________ petition against a debtor ('involuntary _________') in an effort to recoup a portion of what they are owed or initiate a restructuring. In the majority of cases, however, _________ is initiated by the debtor (a 'voluntary _________' that is filed by the bankrupt individual or organization.)

a. 4-4-5 Calendar
b. Bankruptcy
c. Debt settlement
d. 529 plan

26. _________ refers to a tax levied by various jurisdictions on the profits made by companies or associations. It is a tax on the value of the corporation's profits.

The measure of taxable profits varies from country to country.

a. Corporate tax
b. First-mover advantage
c. Trade finance
d. Proxy fight

27. _________ is the imposition of two or more taxes on the same income (in the case of income taxes), asset (in the case of capital taxes), or financial transaction (in the case of sales taxes.) It refers to two distinct situations:

- taxation of dividend income without relief or credit for taxes paid by the company paying the dividend on the income from which the dividend is paid. This arises in the so-called 'classical' system of corporate taxation, used in the United States.
- taxation by two or more countries of the same income, asset or transaction, for example income paid by an entity of one country to a resident of a different country. The double liability is often mitigated by tax treaties between countries.

It is not unusual for a business or individual who is resident in one country to make a taxable gain (earnings, profits) in another. This person may find that he is obliged by domestic laws to pay tax on that gain locally and pay again in the country in which the gain was made. Since this is inequitable, many nations make bilateral _________ agreements with each other.

a. 4-4-5 Calendar
b. 529 plan
c. Double taxation
d. 7-Eleven

28. The phrase _________ refers to the aspect of corporate strategy, corporate finance and management dealing with the buying, selling and combining of different companies that can aid, finance, or help a growing company in a given industry grow rapidly without having to create another business entity.

An acquisition, also known as a takeover, is the buying of one company (the 'target') by another. An acquisition may be friendly or hostile.

a. 4-4-5 Calendar
b. 7-Eleven
c. 529 plan
d. Mergers and acquisitions

1. A _________ is a payment made by a corporation to its shareholder members. When a corporation earns a profit or surplus, that money can be put to two uses: it can either be re-invested in the business (called retained earnings), or it can be paid to the shareholders as a _________. Many corporations retain a portion of their earnings and pay the remainder as a _________.

a. Dividend
b. Dividend puzzle
c. Dividend yield
d. Special dividend

2. _________ is the balance of the amounts of cash being received and paid by a business during a defined period of time, sometimes tied to a specific project. Measurement of _________ can be used

- to evaluate the state or performance of a business or project.
- to determine problems with liquidity. Being profitable does not necessarily mean being liquid. A company can fail because of a shortage of cash, even while profitable.
- to generate project rate of returns. The time of _________s into and out of projects are used as inputs to financial models such as internal rate of return, and net present value.
- to examine income or growth of a business when it is believed that accrual accounting concepts do not represent economic realities. Alternately, _________ can be used to 'validate' the net income generated by accrual accounting.

_________ as a generic term may be used differently depending on context, and certain _________ definitions may be adapted by analysts and users for their own uses. Common terms include operating _________ and free _________.

_________s can be classified into:

1. Operational _________s: Cash received or expended as a result of the company's core business activities.
2. Investment _________s: Cash received or expended through capital expenditure, investments or acquisitions.
3. Financing _________s: Cash received or expended as a result of financial activities, such as interests and dividends.

All three together - the net _________ - are necessary to reconcile the beginning cash balance to the ending cash balance. Loan draw downs or equity injections, that is just shifting of capital but no expenditure as such, are not considered in the net _________.

a. Cash flow
b. Corporate finance
c. Shareholder value
d. Real option

3. _________, refers to consumption opportunity gained by an entity within a specified time frame, which is generally expressed in monetary terms. However, for households and individuals, '_________ is the sum of all the wages, salaries, profits, interests payments, rents and other forms of earnings received... in a given period of time.' For firms, _________ generally refers to net-profit: what remains of revenue after expenses have been subtracted.

a. Income
b. Accrual
c. OIBDA
d. Annual report

4. The _________, in Corporate finance, is a decision made by the directors of a company. It relates to the amount and timing of any cash payments made to the company's stockholders. The decision is an important one for the firm as it may influence its capital structure and stock price.

a. Dividend payout ratio
b. Dividend decision
c. Dividend puzzle
d. Dividend yield

5. An _________ is a tax levied on the financial income of people, corporations, or other legal entities. Various _________ systems exist, with varying degrees of tax incidence. Income taxation can be progressive, proportional, or regressive.

a. ABN Amro
b. AAB
c. A Random Walk Down Wall Street
d. Income tax

6. In economics, business, and accounting, a _________ is the value of money that has been used up to produce something, and hence is not available for use anymore. In business, the _________ may be one of acquisition, in which case the amount of money expended to acquire it is counted as _________. In this case, money is the input that is gone in order to acquire the thing.

a. Sliding scale fees
b. Cost
c. Fixed costs
d. Marginal cost

7. _________ represents the impact on the stock price that investors would cause in reaction to a change in policy of a company.

a. Clientele effect
b. Volatility clustering
c. Trade date
d. Bonus share

8. A _________, in its most general sense, is a solemn promise to engage in or refrain from a specified action.

More specifically, a _________, in contrast to a contract, is a one-way agreement whereby the _________er is the only party bound by the promise. A _________ may have conditions and prerequisites that qualify the undertaking, including the actions of second or third parties, but there is no inherent agreement by such other parties to fulfill those requirements.

a. Partnership
b. Clayton Antitrust Act
c. Covenant
d. Federal Trade Commission Act

9. _________ is that which is owed; usually referencing assets owed, but the term can cover other obligations. In the case of assets, _________ is a means of using future purchasing power in the present before a summation has been earned. Some companies and corporations use _________ as a part of their overall corporate finance strategy.

a. Credit cycle
b. Cross-collateralization
c. Partial Payment
d. Debt

10. _________ is typically a higher ranking stock than voting shares, and its terms are negotiated between the corporation and the investor.

_________ usually carry no voting rights, but may carry superior priority over common stock in the payment of dividends and upon liquidation. _________ may carry a dividend that is paid out prior to any dividends to common stock holders.

a. Second lien loan
b. Follow-on offering
c. Trade-off theory
d. Preferred stock

11. A _________ is an exchange of promises between two or more parties to do an act which is enforceable in a court of law. It is where an unqualified offer meets a qualified acceptance and the parties reach Consensus ad Idem. The parties must have the necessary capacity to _________ and the _________ must not be either trifling, indeterminate, impossible or illegal.

a. 4-4-5 Calendar
b. 7-Eleven
c. Contract
d. 529 plan

12. _________ is the fraction of net income a firm pays to its stockholders in dividends:

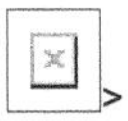
>

The part of the earnings not paid to investors is left for investment to provide for future earnings growth. Investors seeking high current income and limited capital growth prefer companies with high _________. However investors seeking capital growth may prefer lower payout ratio because capital gains are taxed at a lower rate.

a. Dividend puzzle
b. Dividend payout ratio
c. Dividend imputation
d. Dividend yield

13. In business and finance, a _________ (also referred to as equity _________) of stock means a _________ of ownership in a corporation (company.) In the plural, stocks is often used as a synonym for _________s especially in the United States, but it is less commonly used that way outside of North America.

In the United Kingdom, South Africa, and Australia, stock can also refer to completely different financial instruments such as government bonds or, less commonly, to all kinds of marketable securities.

a. Margin
b. Bucket shop
c. Share
d. Procter ' Gamble

14. The key date to remember for dividend paying stocks is the _________. The _________ is different from the record date. The _________ is typically two trading days before the record date.

In order to receive the upcoming dividend payment payout, you must already own or you must purchase the stock prior to the _________. It is important to note that in most countries, when you buy or sell any stock, there is a three trading-day settlement period on your order.

a. Insolvency
b. Asian Financial Crisis
c. Index number
d. Ex-dividend date

15. A _________ is a fungible, negotiable instrument representing financial value. They are broadly categorized into debt securities (such as banknotes, bonds and debentures), and equity securities; e.g., common stocks. The company or other entity issuing the _________ is called the issuer.

a. Security
b. Book entry
c. Securities lending
d. Tracking stock

16. A _________ is an equity investment option offered directly from the underlying company. The investor does not receive quarterly dividends directly as cash; instead, the investor's dividends are directly reinvested in the underlying equity. It should be noted that the investor still must pay tax annually on his or her dividend income, whether it is received or reinvested.

a. Dividend reinvestment plan
b. Dividend puzzle
c. Dividend payout ratio
d. Dividend decision

17. A _________ is a profit that results from investments into a capital asset, such as stocks, bonds or real estate, which exceeds the purchase price. It is the difference between a higher selling price and a lower purchase price, resulting in a financial gain for the seller. Conversely, a capital loss arises if the proceeds from the sale of a capital asset are less than the purchase price.

a. Capital gain
b. Tax brackets
c. Payroll tax
d. Capital gains tax

18. A _________ or stock divide increases or decreases the number of shares in a public company. The price is adjusted such that the before and after market capitalization of the company remains the same and dilution does not occur. Options and warrants are included.

a. Stock split
b. Contract for difference
c. Stop order
d. Stop price

19. On a stock exchange, a _________ is the opposite of a stock split, i.e. a stock merge - a reduction in the number of shares and an accompanying increase in the share price. The ratio is also reversed: 1-for-2, 1-for-3 and so on.

There is a stigma attached to doing this so it is not initiated without very good reason.

a. Correlation trading
b. Conglomerate merger
c. Trade date
d. Reverse stock split

20. _________ are those dividends paid out in form of additional stock shares of the issuing corporation or other corporation They are usually issued in proportion to shares owned (for example for every 100 shares of stock owned, 5% stock dividend will yield 5 extra shares). If this payment involves the issue of new shares, this is very similar to a stock split in that it increases the total number of shares while lowering the price of each share and does not change the market capitalization or the total value of the shares held

a. The Hong Kong Securities Institute
b. Stock or scrip dividends
c. Database auditing
d. Time-based currency

21. In some countries, including the United States and the United Kingdom, corporations can buy back their own stock in a share repurchase, also known as a _________ or share buyback. There has been a meteoric rise in the use of share repurchases in the U.S. in the past twenty years, from $5b in 1980 to $349b in 2005. A share repurchase distributes cash to existing shareholders in exchange for a fraction of the firm's outstanding equity.

a. Stockholder
b. Stock repurchase
c. Trading curb
d. Common stock

22. _________ is a corporate finance term denoting a type of takeover bid. The _________ is a public, open offer or invitation (usually announced in a newspaper advertisement) by a prospective acquirer to all stockholders of a publicly traded corporation (the target corporation) to tender their stock for sale at a specified price during a specified time, subject to the tendering of a minimum and maximum number of shares. In a _________, the bidder contacts shareholders directly; the directors of the company may or may not have endorsed the _________ proposal.

a. Follow-on offering
b. Cash is king
c. Shareholder value
d. Tender offer

23. In corporate finance, _________ is an estimate of true economic profit after making corrective adjustments to GAAP accounting, including deducting the opportunity cost of equity capital. GAAP is estimated to ignore US$300 billion in shareholder opportunity costs. _________ can be measured as Net Operating Profit After Taxes(or NOPAT) less the money cost of capital.

a. AAB
b. A Random Walk Down Wall Street
c. ABN Amro
d. Economic value added

24. _________ refers to the additional value of a commodity over the cost of commodities used to produce it from the previous stage of production. An example is the price of gasoline at the pump over the price of the oil in it. In national accounts used in macroeconomics, it refers to the contribution of the factors of production, i.e., land, labor, and capital goods, to raising the value of a product and corresponds to the incomes received by the owners of these factors.

a. Value added
b. Deregulation
c. Demand shock
d. Supply shock

1. _________ is a financial metric which represents operating liquidity available to a business. Along with fixed assets such as plant and equipment, _________ is considered a part of operating capital. It is calculated as current assets minus current liabilities.

a. 4-4-5 Calendar
b. 529 plan
c. Working capital management
d. Working capital

2. Decisions relating to working capital and short term financing are referred to as _________. These involve managing the relationship between a firm's short-term assets and its short-term liabilities. The goal of _________ is to ensure that the firm is able to continue its operations and that it has sufficient cash flow to satisfy both maturing short-term debt and upcoming operational expenses.

a. Working capital management
b. 529 plan
c. Working capital
d. 4-4-5 Calendar

3. In economics, the _________ is one of the two primary components of the balance of payments, the other being the capital account. It is the sum of the balance of trade (exports minus imports of goods and services), net factor income (such as interest and dividends) and net transfer payments (such as foreign aid.)

>

The _________ balance is one of two major metrics of the nature of a country's foreign trade (the other being the net capital outflow).

a. Cash budget
b. Consols
c. Current account
d. Rights issue

4. _________ or financing is to provide capital (funds), which means money for a project, a person, a business or any other private or public institutions.

Those funds can be allocated for either short term or long term purposes. The health fund is a new way of _________ private healthcare centers.

a. Synthetic CDO
b. Proxy fight
c. Product life cycle
d. Funding

5. _________, in bookkeeping, refers to assets, liabilities, income, and expenses recorded on individual pages of the so called book of final entry or ledger. Changes in _________ value are made by chronologically posting debit (DR) and credit (CR) entries to its page. Examples of _________s are cash, _________s receivable, mortgages, loans, land and buildings, common stock, sales, services provided, wages, and payroll overhead.

a. Accretion
b. Account
c. Alpha
d. Option

6. In economics, the concept of the _________ refers to the decision-making time frame of a firm in which at least one factor of production is fixed. Costs which are fixed in the _________ have no impact on a firms decisions. For example a firm can raise output by increasing the amount of labour through overtime.

a. Long-run
b. Short-run
c. 529 plan
d. 4-4-5 Calendar

7. In business and accounting, _________s are everything of value that is owned by a person or company. The balance sheet of a firm records the monetary value of the _________s owned by the firm. The two major _________ classes are tangible _________s and intangible _________s.

a. EBITDA
b. Accounts payable
c. Income
d. Asset

8. _________ is the provision of resources (such as granting a loan) by one party to another party where that second party does not reimburse the first party immediately, thereby generating a debt, and instead arranges either to repay or return those resources (or material(s) of equal value) at a later date. The first party is called a creditor, also known as a lender, while the second party is called a debtor, also known as a borrower.

Movements of financial capital are normally dependent on either _________ or equity transfers.

a. Warrant
b. Credit
c. Comparable
d. Clearing house

9. In accounting, a _________ is an asset on the balance sheet which is expected to be sold or otherwise used up in the near future, usually within one year, or one business cycle - whichever is longer. Typical _________s include cash, cash equivalents, accounts receivable, inventory, the portion of prepaid accounts which will be used within a year, and short-term investments.

On the balance sheet, assets will typically be classified into _________s and long-term assets.

a. Historical cost
b. Write-off
c. Long-term liabilities
d. Current asset

10. The _________ measures how long an investment with suppliers deprives a firm of cash -- it is (in the generic case of a retailer) the time between disbursement for inventory and collection on its sale. Thus, the _________ measures how risky it would be to increase this investment with suppliers in the course of expanding customer sales. However, shortening the _________ creates its own risks: while a firm could even achieve a negative _________ by collecting from customers before paying suppliers, a policy of strict collections and lax payments is not always sustainable.

a. Return on sales
b. Return on capital employed
c. Price/cash flow ratio
d. Cash conversion cycle

11. _________ is a life of security. It may also refer to the final payment date of a loan or other financial instrument, at which point all remaining interest and principal is due to be paid.

1, 3, 6 months _________ band can be calculated by using 30-day per month periods.

a. Replacement cost
b. Primary market
c. False billing
d. Maturity

12. _________ is that which is owed; usually referencing assets owed, but the term can cover other obligations. In the case of assets, _________ is a means of using future purchasing power in the present before a summation has been earned. Some companies and corporations use _________ as a part of their overall corporate finance strategy.

a. Cross-collateralization
b. Credit cycle
c. Partial Payment
d. Debt

13. _________ is a cornerstone of accrual accounting together with revenue recognition. They both determine the point, at which expenses and revenues are recognized. According to the principle, expenses are recognized when they are (1) incurred and (2) offset against recognized revenues, which were generated from those expenses (related on the cause-and-effect basis), no matter when cash is paid out.

a. Pro forma
b. Gross sales
c. Retained earnings
d. Matching principle

14. In economic models, the _________ time frame assumes no fixed factors of production. Firms can enter or leave the marketplace, and the cost (and availability) of land, labor, raw materials, and capital goods can be assumed to vary. In contrast, in the short-run time frame, certain factors are assumed to be fixed, because there is not sufficient time for them to change.

a. 4-4-5 Calendar
b. 529 plan
c. Short-run
d. Long-run

15. Accrual, in accounting, describes the accounting method known as _________, whereby revenues and expenses are recognized when they are accrued, i.e. accumulated (earned or incurred), regardless when the actual cash is received or paid out.

E.g. a company delivers a product to a customer who will pay for it 30 days later in the next fiscal year starting a week after the delivery. The company recognizes the proceeds as a revenue in its current income statement still for the fiscal year of the delivery, even though it will get paid in cash during the following accounting period.

a. ABN Amro
b. AAB
c. A Random Walk Down Wall Street
d. Accrual basis

16. _________ is a file or account that contains money that a person or company owes to suppliers, but hasn't paid yet (a form of debt.) When you receive an invoice you add it to the file, and then you remove it when you pay. Thus, the A/P is a form of credit that suppliers offer to their purchasers by allowing them to pay for a product or service after it has already been received.

a. Outstanding balance
b. Accounts payable
c. Earnings before interest, taxes, depreciation and amortization
d. Accrual

17. _________ exists when one firm provides goods or services to a customer with an agreement to bill them later, or receive a shipment or service from a supplier under an agreement to pay them later. It can be viewed as an essential element of capitalization in an operating business because it can reduce the required capital investment to operate the business if it is managed properly. _________ is the largest use of capital for a majority of business to business (B2B) sellers in the United States and is a critical source of capital for a majority of all businesses.

a. 4-4-5 Calendar
b. 529 plan
c. Going concern
d. Trade credit

18. A '_________' is a 'Charge' that is paid to obtain the right to delay a payment. Essentially, the payer purchases the right to make a given payment in the future instead of in the Present. The '_________', or 'Charge' that must be paid to delay the payment, is simply the difference between what the payment amount would be if it were paid in the present and what the payment amount would be paid if it were paid in the future.

a. Risk modeling
b. Value at risk
c. Risk aversion
d. Discount

19. A _________ (U.S.), or credit reference agency (UK) is a company that collects information from various sources and provides consumer credit information on individual consumers for a variety of uses. This helps lenders assess credit worthiness, the ability to pay back a loan, and can affect the interest rate and other terms of a loan. Interest rates are not the same for everyone, but instead can be based on risk-based pricing, a form of price discrimination based on the different expected risks of different borrowers, as set out in their credit rating.

a. Probability of default
b. Reserve requirement
c. Wall Street Journal prime rate
d. Credit bureau

20. A _________ is any credit facility extended to a business by a bank or financial institution. A _________ may take several forms such as cash credit, overdraft, demand loan, export packing credit, term loan, discounting or purchase of commercial bills etc. It is like an account that can readily be tapped into if the need arises or not touched at all and saved for emergencies.

a. Line of credit
b. Default Notice
c. Cash credit
d. Debt-snowball method

21. A _________, referred to as a note payable in accounting, is a contract where one party (the maker or issuer) makes an unconditional promise in writing to pay a sum of money to the other (the payee), either at a fixed or determinable future time or on demand of the payee, under specific terms. They differ from IOUs in that they contain a specific promise to pay, rather than simply acknowledging that a debt exists.

The terms of a note typically include the principal amount, the interest rate if any, and the maturity date.

a. Financial plan
b. Credit repair software
c. Title loan
d. Promissory note

22. _________ is a term applied in many countries to a reference interest rate used by banks. The term originally indicated the rate of interest at which banks lent to favored customers, i.e., those with high credibility, though this is no longer always the case. Some variable interest rates may be expressed as a percentage above or below _________.

a. Reserve requirement
b. Prime rate
c. Time deposit
d. Credit bureau

23. _________ is a type of credit that does not have a fixed number of payments, in contrast to installment credit. Examples of _________s used by consumers include credit cards. Corporate _________ facilities are typically used to provide liquidity for a company's day-to-day operations.

a. Reverse stock split
b. Commercial finance
c. Package loan
d. Revolving credit

24. In the global money market, _________ is an unsecured promissory note with a fixed maturity of one to 270 days. _________ is a money-market security issued (sold) by large banks and corporations to get money to meet short term debt obligations (for example, payroll), and is only backed by an issuing bank or corporation's promise to pay the face amount on the maturity date specified on the note. Since it is not backed by collateral, only firms with excellent credit ratings from a recognized rating agency will be able to sell their _________ at a reasonable price.

a. Trade-off theory
b. Financial distress
c. Book building
d. Commercial paper

25. _________ is one of a series of accounting transactions dealing with the billing of customers who owe money to a person, company or organization for goods and services that have been provided to the customer. In most business entities this is typically done by generating an invoice and mailing or electronically delivering it to the customer, who in turn must pay it within an established timeframe called credit or payment terms.

An example of a common payment term is Net 30, meaning payment is due in the amount of the invoice 30 days from the date of invoice.

a. Income
b. Accounts receivable
c. Accounting methods
d. Impaired asset

26. _________ is a financial transaction whereby a business sells its accounts receivable (i.e., invoices) at a discount. _________ differs from a bank loan in three main ways. First, the emphasis is on the value of the receivables (essentially a financial asset), not the firm's credit worthiness.

a. Debt-for-equity swap
b. Factoring
c. Financial Literacy Month
d. Credit card balance transfer

27. _________ is a list for goods and materials held available in stock by a business. It is also used for a list of the contents of a household and for a list for testamentary purposes of the possessions of someone who has died. In accounting _________ is considered an asset.

a. AAB
b. A Random Walk Down Wall Street
c. ABN Amro
d. Inventory

28. In United States banking, _________ is a marketing term for certain services offered primarily to larger business customers. It may be used to describe all bank accounts (such as checking accounts) provided to businesses of a certain size, but it is more often used to describe specific services such as cash concentration, zero balance accounting, and automated clearing house facilities. Sometimes, private banking customers are given _________ services.

a. Profitability index
b. Capitalization rate
c. Global tactical asset allocation
d. Cash management

29. In law, a _________ is a form of security interest granted over an item of property to secure the payment of a debt or performance of some other obligation. The owner of the property, who grants the _________, is referred to as the lienor and the person who has the benefit of the _________ is referred to as the _________ee.

The etymological root is: Anglo-French _________, loyen bond, restraint, from Latin ligamen, from ligare to bind.

a. Family and Medical Leave Act
b. Sarbanes-Oxley Act
c. Joint venture
d. Lien

30. _________ is the demand for financial assets, such as securities, money or foreign currency; it is money people want in case of emergency.

In economic theory, specifically Keynesian economics, _________ is one of the determinants of demand for money (and credit), the others being transactions demand and Speculative demand.

a. 4-4-5 Calendar
b. 529 plan
c. Precautionary demand
d. 7-Eleven

31. _________ is the demand for financial assets, such as securities, money or foreign currency that is not dictated by real transactions such as trade, or financing.

The need for cash to take advantage of investment opportunities that may arise.

In economic theory, specifically Keynesian economics, _________ is one of the determinants of demand for money (and credit), the others being transactions demand and precautionary demand.

a. 4-4-5 Calendar
b. 7-Eleven
c. Speculative demand
d. 529 plan

32. _________ is the demand for financial assets, e.g., securities, money or foreign currency. It is used for purposes of business transactions and personal consumption.

The need to accommodate a firm's expected cash transactions.

a. Transactions demand
b. 4-4-5 Calendar
c. 7-Eleven
d. 529 plan

33. A _________ is a pool of assets forming an independent legal entity that are bought with the contributions to a pension plan for the exclusive purpose of financing pension plan benefits.

_________s are important shareholders of listed and private companies. They are especially important to the stock market where large institutional investors like the Ontario Teachers' Pension Plan dominate.

a. Limited liability company
b. Leverage
c. Leveraged buyout
d. Pension fund

34. A _________ is a business that pursues payments on debts owed by individuals or businesses. Most collection agencies operate as agents of creditors and collect debts for a fee or percentage of the total amount owed. Some agencies, sometimes referred to as 'debt buyers', purchase debts from creditors for a fraction of the value of the debt and pursue the debtor for the full balance.

a. Partial Payment
b. Collection agency
c. Guaranteed consumer funding
d. Commercial hard money

35. _________ are securities that can be easily converted into cash. Such securities will generally have highly liquid markets allowing the security to be sold at a reasonable price very quickly.This is a usual feature in real estate .

a. Book entry
b. Tracking stock
c. Securities lending
d. Marketable

36. The institution most often referenced by the word '_________' is a public or publicly traded _________, the shares of which are traded on a public stock exchange (e.g., the New York Stock Exchange or Nasdaq in the United States) where shares of stock of _________s are bought and sold by and to the general public. Most of the largest businesses in the world are publicly traded _________s. However, the majority of _________s are said to be closely held, privately held or close _________s, meaning that no ready market exists for the trading of shares.

a. Protect
b. Depository Trust Company
c. Federal Home Loan Mortgage Corporation
d. Corporation

37. A _________ is a fungible, negotiable instrument representing financial value. They are broadly categorized into debt securities (such as banknotes, bonds and debentures), and equity securities; e.g., common stocks. The company or other entity issuing the _________ is called the issuer.

a. Security
b. Book entry
c. Securities lending
d. Tracking stock

38. The free _________ of a public company is an estimate of the proportion of shares that are not held by large owners and that are not stock with sales restrictions (restricted stock that cannot be sold until they become unrestricted stock.)

The free _________ or a public _________ is usually defined as being all shares held by investors other than:

- shares held by owners owning more than 5% of all shares (those could be institutional investors, 'strategic shareholders,' founders, executives, and other insiders' holdings)
- restricted stocks (granted to executives that can be, but don't have to be, registered insiders)
- insider holdings (it is assumed that insiders hold stock for the very long term)

The free _________ is an important criterion in quoting a share on the stock market.

To _________ a company means to list its shares on a public stock exchange through an initial public offering (or 'flotation'.)

- Open market
- Outstanding shares
- Market capitalization
- Public _________ *loat*
- Reverse takeover

.

a. Synthetic CDO
b. Trade finance
c. Golden parachute
d. Float

39. In economics, business, and accounting, a _________ is the value of money that has been used up to produce something, and hence is not available for use anymore. In business, the _________ may be one of acquisition, in which case the amount of money expended to acquire it is counted as _________. In this case, money is the input that is gone in order to acquire the thing.

a. Fixed costs
b. Marginal cost
c. Sliding scale fees
d. Cost

40. The _________ is the level of inventory when a fresh order should be made with suppliers to bring the inventory up by the Economic order quantity ('EOQ'.)

The _________ for replenishment of stock occurs when the level of inventory drops down to zero. In view of instantaneous replenishment of stock the level of inventory jumps to the original level from zero level.

a. 4-4-5 Calendar
b. Reorder point
c. 7-Eleven
d. 529 plan

41. _________ is a term used by inventory specialists to describe a level of extra stock that is maintained below the cycle stock to buffer against stockouts. _________ exists to counter uncertainties in supply and demand. _________ is defined as extra units of inventory carried as protection against possible stockouts .(shortfall in raw material or packaging.)

a. Golden parachute
b. Counting house
c. Funding
d. Safety stock

42. In business and finance, a _________ (also referred to as equity _________) of stock means a _________ of ownership in a corporation (company.) In the plural, stocks is often used as a synonym for _________s especially in the United States, but it is less commonly used that way outside of North America.

In the United Kingdom, South Africa, and Australia, stock can also refer to completely different financial instruments such as government bonds or, less commonly, to all kinds of marketable securities.

a. Margin
b. Bucket shop
c. Procter ' Gamble
d. Share

1. _________ is the task of determining how a business will afford to achieve its strategic goals and objectives. Usually, a company creates a Financial Plan immediately after the vision and objectives have been set. The Financial Plan describes each of the activities, resources, equipment and materials that are needed to achieve these objectives, as well as the timeframes involved.

a. Financial planning
b. Corporate Transparency
c. Management by exception
d. Performance measurement

2. In general usage, a _________ can be a budget, a plan for spending and saving future income. This plan allocates future income to various types of expenses, such as rent or utilities, and also reserves some income for short-term and long-term savings. A _________ can also be an investment plan, which allocates savings to various assets or projects expected to produce future income, such as a new business or product line, shares in an existing business, or real estate.

a. Credit repair software
b. Financial plan
c. Title loan
d. Promissory note

3. _________ or financing is to provide capital (funds), which means money for a project, a person, a business or any other private or public institutions.

Those funds can be allocated for either short term or long term purposes. The health fund is a new way of _________ private healthcare centers.

a. Product life cycle
b. Proxy fight
c. Synthetic CDO
d. Funding

4. _________ is a process by which a firm can obtain the use of a certain fixed assets for which it must pay a series of contractual, periodic, tax deductable payments. The lessee is the receiver of the services or the assets under the lease contract and the lessor is the owner of the assets. The relationship between the tenant and the landlord is called a tenancy, and can be for a fixed or an indefinite period of time (called the term of the lease).

a. Leasing
b. Royalties
c. Foreign Corrupt Practices Act
d. Quiet period

5. The _________ is the amount of time an organization will look into the future when preparing a strategic plan. Many commercial companies use a five-year _________, but other organizations such as the Forestry Commission in the UK have to use a much longer _________ to form effective plans.

a. Trade finance
b. Planning horizon
c. Debtor-in-possession financing
d. First-mover advantage

6. _________ is an organization's process of defining its strategy and making decisions on allocating its resources to pursue this strategy, including its capital and people. Various business analysis techniques can be used in _________, including SWOT analysis (Strengths, Weaknesses, Opportunities, and Threats) and PEST analysis (Political, Economic, Social, and Technological analysis) or STEER analysis involving Socio-cultural, Technological, Economic, Ecological, and Regulatory factors and EPISTEL (Environment, Political, Informatic, Social, Technological, Economic and Legal)

_________ is the formal consideration of an organization's future course. All _________ deals with at least one of three key questions:

1. 'What do we do?'
2. 'For whom do we do it?'
3. 'How do we excel?'

In business _________, the third question is better phrased 'How can we beat or avoid competition?'. (Bradford and Duncan, page 1.)

a. 4-4-5 Calendar
b. 529 plan
c. Strategic planning
d. 7-Eleven

7. An _________ is a subset of strategic work plan. It describes short-term ways of achieving milestones and explains how, or what portion of, a strategic plan will be put into operation during a given operational period, in the case of commercial application, a fiscal year or another given budgetary term. An operational plan is the basis for, and justification of an annual operating budget request.

a. ABN Amro
b. AAB
c. Operational planning
d. A Random Walk Down Wall Street

8. _________ is the maximum rate at which a company can grow revenue without having to invest new equity capital. If a company earns a 15% return on equity (ROE), it can grow 15% simply by reinvesting all the earnings in new opportunities and maintaining a stable debt to equity ratio. In order to grow faster, the company would have to invest more equity capital or increase its financial leverage.

a. Return on capital employed
b. Sustainable growth rate
c. Price/cash flow ratio
d. Current ratio

9. _________ plant, and equipment, is a term used in accountancy for assets and property which cannot easily be converted into cash. This can be compared with current assets such as cash or bank accounts, which are described as liquid assets. In most cases, only tangible assets are referred to as fixed.

a. Petty cash
b. Fixed asset
c. Remittance advice
d. Percentage of Completion

10. In business and accounting, _________s are everything of value that is owned by a person or company. The balance sheet of a firm records the monetary value of the _________s owned by the firm. The two major _________ classes are tangible _________s and intangible _________s.

a. Accounts payable
b. Asset
c. EBITDA
d. Income

11. Working capital requirements of a business should be monitored at all times to ensure that there are sufficient funds available to meet short-term expenses.

The _________ is basically a detailed plan that shows all expected sources and uses of cash

a. Mitigating Control
b. Rate of return
c. Cash budget
d. Loans and interest, in Judaism

12. _________ is a fee paid on borrowed assets. It is the price paid for the use of borrowed money , or, money earned by deposited funds . Assets that are sometimes lent with _________ include money, shares, consumer goods through hire purchase, major assets such as aircraft, and even entire factories in finance lease arrangements.

a. Insolvency
b. A Random Walk Down Wall Street
c. AAB
d. Interest

13. _________ is that which is owed; usually referencing assets owed, but the term can cover other obligations. In the case of assets, _________ is a means of using future purchasing power in the present before a summation has been earned. Some companies and corporations use _________ as a part of their overall corporate finance strategy.

a. Cross-collateralization
b. Credit cycle
c. Partial Payment
d. Debt

14. _________ is a process of analyzing possible future events by considering alternative possible outcomes (scenarios.) The analysis is designed to allow improved decision-making by allowing consideration of outcomes and their implications.

For example, in economics and finance, a financial institution might attempt to forecast several possible scenarios for the economy (e.g. rapid growth, moderate growth, slow growth) and it might also attempt to forecast financial market returns (for bonds, stocks and cash) in each of those scenarios.

a. 4-4-5 Calendar
b. 529 plan
c. Detection Risk
d. Scenario analysis

15. _________ is a legally declared inability or impairment of ability of an individual or organization to pay their creditors. Creditors may file a _________ petition against a debtor ('involuntary _________') in an effort to recoup a portion of what they are owed or initiate a restructuring. In the majority of cases, however, _________ is initiated by the debtor (a 'voluntary _________' that is filed by the bankrupt individual or organization.)

a. 529 plan
b. 4-4-5 Calendar
c. Debt settlement
d. Bankruptcy

1. The phrase _________ refers to the aspect of corporate strategy, corporate finance and management dealing with the buying, selling and combining of different companies that can aid, finance, or help a growing company in a given industry grow rapidly without having to create another business entity.

An acquisition, also known as a takeover, is the buying of one company (the 'target') by another. An acquisition may be friendly or hostile.

a. 529 plan
b. 4-4-5 Calendar
c. Mergers and acquisitions
d. 7-Eleven

2. _________ is the imposition of two or more taxes on the same income (in the case of income taxes), asset (in the case of capital taxes), or financial transaction (in the case of sales taxes.) It refers to two distinct situations:

- taxation of dividend income without relief or credit for taxes paid by the company paying the dividend on the income from which the dividend is paid. This arises in the so-called 'classical' system of corporate taxation, used in the United States.
- taxation by two or more countries of the same income, asset or transaction, for example income paid by an entity of one country to a resident of a different country. The double liability is often mitigated by tax treaties between countries.

It is not unusual for a business or individual who is resident in one country to make a taxable gain (earnings, profits) in another. This person may find that he is obliged by domestic laws to pay tax on that gain locally and pay again in the country in which the gain was made. Since this is inequitable, many nations make bilateral _________ agreements with each other.

a. 4-4-5 Calendar
b. 7-Eleven
c. 529 plan
d. Double taxation

3. _________ is the corporate management term for the act of reorganizing the legal, ownership, operational, or other structures of a company for the purpose of making it more profitable or better organized for its present needs. Alternate reasons for restructing include a change of ownership or ownership structure, demerger repositioning debt _________ and financial _________.

a. Day trading
b. Cross-border leasing
c. Restructuring
d. Concentrated stock

4. _________ or amalgamation is the act of merging many things into one. In business, it often refers to the mergers or acquisitions of many smaller companies into much larger ones. The financial accounting term of _________ refers to the aggregated financial statements of a group company as consolidated account.

a. Write-off
b. Cost of goods sold
c. Retained earnings
d. Consolidation

5. In finance, a _________ is a debt security, in which the authorized issuer owes the holders a debt and, depending on the terms of the _________, is obliged to pay interest (the coupon) and/or to repay the principal at a later date, termed maturity.

Thus a _________ is a loan: the issuer is the borrower, the _________ holder is the lender, and the coupon is the interest. _________s provide the borrower with external funds to finance long-term investments, or, in the case of government _________s, to finance current expenditure.

a. Puttable bond
b. Bond
c. Convertible bond
d. Catastrophe bonds

6. In finance, a _________ (non-investment grade bond, speculative grade bond or junk bond) is a bond that is rated below investment grade at the time of purchase. These bonds have a higher risk of default or other adverse credit events, but typically pay higher yields than better quality bonds in order to make them attractive to investors.

a. Sharpe ratio
b. Private equity
c. Volatility
d. High yield bond

7. A mutual shareholder or _________ is an individual or company (including a corporation) that legally owns one or more shares of stock in a joint stock company. A company's shareholders collectively own that company. Thus, the typical goal of such companies is to enhance shareholder value.

a. Stockholder
b. Trading curb
c. Limit order
d. Stock market bubble

8. A _________ is officially defined as being 'any merger that is not horizontal or vertical; in general, it is the combination of firms in different industries or firms operating in different geographic areas'. _________s can serve various purposes, including extending corporate territories and extending a product range. One example of a _________ was the merger between the Walt Disney Company and the American Broadcasting Company.

a. Redemption value
b. Volatility clustering
c. Refunding
d. Conglomerate merger

9. In economics, a _________ is the combination of two or more firms competing in the same market with the same good or service.

a. 4-4-5 Calendar
b. Horizontal merger
c. Fixed exchange rate system
d. Passive income

10. _________ is the balance of the amounts of cash being received and paid by a business during a defined period of time, sometimes tied to a specific project. Measurement of _________ can be used

- to evaluate the state or performance of a business or project.
- to determine problems with liquidity. Being profitable does not necessarily mean being liquid. A company can fail because of a shortage of cash, even while profitable.
- to generate project rate of returns. The time of _________s into and out of projects are used as inputs to financial models such as internal rate of return, and net present value.
- to examine income or growth of a business when it is believed that accrual accounting concepts do not represent economic realities. Alternately, _________ can be used to 'validate' the net income generated by accrual accounting.

_________ as a generic term may be used differently depending on context, and certain _________ definitions may be adapted by analysts and users for their own uses. Common terms include operating _________ and free _________.

_________s can be classified into:

1. Operational _________s: Cash received or expended as a result of the company's core business activities.
2. Investment _________s: Cash received or expended through capital expenditure, investments or acquisitions.
3. Financing _________s: Cash received or expended as a result of financial activities, such as interests and dividends.

All three together - the net _________ - are necessary to reconcile the beginning cash balance to the ending cash balance. Loan draw downs or equity injections, that is just shifting of capital but no expenditure as such, are not considered in the net _________.

a. Corporate finance
b. Real option
c. Shareholder value
d. Cash flow

11. _________, known in the United States as antitrust law, has three main elements:

- prohibiting agreements or practices that restrict free trading and competition between business entities. This includes in particular the repression of cartels.
- banning abusive behaviour by a firm dominating a market, or anti-competitive practices that tend to lead to such a dominant position. Practices controlled in this way may include predatory pricing, tying, price gouging, refusal to deal, and many others.
- supervising the mergers and acquisitions of large corporations, including some joint ventures. Transactions that are considered to threaten the competitive process can be prohibited altogether, or approved subject to 'remedies' such as an obligation to divest part of the merged business or to offer licences or access to facilities to enable other businesses to continue competing.

The substance and practice of _________ varies from jurisdiction to jurisdiction. Protecting the interests of consumers (consumer welfare) and ensuring that entrepreneurs have an opportunity to compete in the market economy are often treated as important objectives. _________ is closely connected with law on deregulation of access to markets, state aids and subsidies, the privatisation of state owned assets and the establishment of independent sector regulators. In recent decades, _________ has been viewed as a way to provide better public services.

a. Joint venture
b. Fair Labor Standards Act
c. Securities Investor Protection Act
d. Competition law

12. _________ in finance is a risk management technique, related to hedging, that mixes a wide variety of investments within a portfolio. Because the fluctuations of a single security have less impact on a diverse portfolio, _________ minimizes the risk from any one investment.

A simple example of _________ is the following: On a particular island the entire economy consists of two companies: one that sells umbrellas and another that sells sunscreen.

a. 4-4-5 Calendar
b. 7-Eleven
c. 529 plan
d. Diversification

13. In business and accounting, _________s are everything of value that is owned by a person or company. The balance sheet of a firm records the monetary value of the _________s owned by the firm. The two major _________ classes are tangible _________s and intangible _________s.

a. Asset
b. Accounts payable
c. Income
d. EBITDA

14. _________, in microeconomics, are the cost advantages that a business obtains due to expansion. _________ may be utilized by any size firm expanding its scale of operation.

a. Economies of scale
b. Employee Retirement Income Security Act
c. Articles of incorporation
d. Uniform Commercial Code

15. A _________ is a company that owns other companies' outstanding stock. It usually refers to a company which does not produce goods or services itself, rather its only purpose is owning shares of other companies. They allow the reduction of risk for the owners and can allow the ownership and control of a number of different companies.

a. Holding company
b. Privately held company
c. MRU Holdings
d. Federal National Mortgage Association

16. In mathematics, _________ are used in the study of chance and probability. They were developed to assist in the analysis of games of chance, stochastic events, and the results of scientific experiments by capturing only the mathematical properties necessary to answer probabilistic questions. Further formalizations have firmly grounded the entity in the theoretical domains of mathematics by making use of measure theory.

a. Variance
b. Standard deviation
c. Random variables
d. Monte Carlo methods

17. A '_________' is a 'Charge' that is paid to obtain the right to delay a payment. Essentially, the payer purchases the right to make a given payment in the future instead of in the Present. The '_________', or 'Charge' that must be paid to delay the payment, is simply the difference between what the payment amount would be if it were paid in the present and what the payment amount would be paid if it were paid in the future.

a. Value at risk
b. Risk modeling
c. Discount
d. Risk aversion

18. The _________ is an interest rate a central bank charges depository institutions that borrow reserves from it.

The term _________ has two meanings:

- the same as interest rate; the term 'discount' does not refer to the meaning of the word, but to the purpose of using the quantity, such as computations of present value, e.g. net present value / discounted cash flow

- the annual effective _________, which is the annual interest divided by the capital including that interest; this rate is lower than the interest rate; it corresponds to using the value after a year as the nominal value, and seeing the initial value as the nominal value minus a discount; it is used for Treasury Bills and similar financial instruments

The annual effective _________ is the annual interest divided by the capital including that interest, which is the interest rate divided by 100% plus the interest rate. It is the annual discount factor to be applied to the future cash flow, to find the discount, subtracted from a future value to find the value one year earlier.

For example, suppose there is a government bond that sells for $95 and pays $100 in a year's time.

a. Black-Scholes
b. Fisher equation
c. Stochastic volatility
d. Discount rate

19. _________ is an economic concept with commonplace familiarity. It is the price that a good or service is offered at, or will fetch, in the marketplace. It is of interest mainly in the study of microeconomics.

a. Delta hedging
b. Market price
c. Central Securities Depository
d. Convertible arbitrage

20. _________, refers to consumption opportunity gained by an entity within a specified time frame, which is generally expressed in monetary terms. However, for households and individuals, '_________ is the sum of all the wages, salaries, profits, interests payments, rents and other forms of earnings received... in a given period of time.' For firms, _________ generally refers to net-profit: what remains of revenue after expenses have been subtracted.

a. Income
b. Accrual
c. Annual report
d. OIBDA

21. In finance, the _________ (continuing value or horizon value) of a security is the present value at a future point in time of all future cash flows when we expect stable growth rate forever. It is most often used in multi-stage discounted cash flow analysis, and allows for the limitation of cash flow projections to a several-year period. Forecasting results beyond such a period is impractical and exposes such projections to a variety of risks limiting their validity, primarily the great uncertainty involved in predicting industry and macroeconomic conditions beyond a few years.

a. Terminal value
b. Negative gearing
c. Refinancing risk
d. Discounted cash flow

22. A _________ is a fungible, negotiable instrument representing financial value. They are broadly categorized into debt securities (such as banknotes, bonds and debentures), and equity securities; e.g., common stocks. The company or other entity issuing the _________ is called the issuer.

a. Securities lending
b. Book entry
c. Tracking stock
d. Security

23. In Modern Portfolio Theory, the _________ is the graphical representation of the Capital Asset Pricing Model. It displays the expected rate of return for an overall market as a function of systematic (non-diversifiable) risk (beta.)

The Y-Intercept (beta=0) of the _________ is equal to the risk-free interest rate.

a. Rebalancing
b. Divestment
c. Certificate in Investment Performance Measurement
d. Security market line

24. In finance, _________ refers to the way a corporation finances its assets through some combination of equity, debt, or hybrid securities. A firm's _________ is then the composition or 'structure' of its liabilities. For example, a firm that sells $20 billion in equity and $80 billion in debt is said to be 20% equity-financed and 80% debt-financed.

a. Capital structure
b. Book building
c. Market for corporate control
d. Rights issue

25. In business, a _________ is the purchase of one company (the target) by another (the acquirer or bidder). In the UK the term refers to the acquisition of a public company whose shares are listed on a stock exchange, in contrast to the acquisition of a private company.

Before a bidder makes an offer for another company, it usually first informs that company's board of directors.

a. Stock swap
b. 4-4-5 Calendar
c. Takeover
d. 529 plan

26. _________ is money paid by a company (or allied company or individual) to acquire its own shares of stock from a shareholder who is threatening to take control of, or unwanted influence of, the company.

The term is a neologism combining the terms greenback and blackmail, invented by journalists and commentators who saw the practices of corporate raiders as a form of blackmail. The target company is financially held hostage, and is legally forced to pay the _________er to go away.

a. 529 plan
b. Greenmail
c. Stock swap
d. 4-4-5 Calendar

27. A _________ is an agreement between a company and an employee (usually upper executive) specifying that the employee will receive certain significant benefits if employment is terminated. Sometimes, certain conditions, typically a change in company ownership, must be met, but often the cause of termination is unspecified. These benefits may include severance pay, cash bonuses, stock options, or other benefits.

a. Market capitalization
b. Trade finance
c. Golden parachute
d. Debtor-in-possession financing

28. A _________ occurs when a financial sponsor acquires a controlling interest in a company's equity and where a significant percentage of the purchase price is financed through leverage (borrowing.) The assets of the acquired company are used as collateral for the borrowed capital, sometimes with assets of the acquiring company. The bonds or other paper issued for _________s are commonly considered not to be investment grade because of the significant risks involved.

a. Leverage
b. Limited partnership
c. Pension fund
d. Leveraged buyout

29. In business and finance, a _________ (also referred to as equity _________) of stock means a _________ of ownership in a corporation (company.) In the plural, stocks is often used as a synonym for _________s especially in the United States, but it is less commonly used that way outside of North America.

In the United Kingdom, South Africa, and Australia, stock can also refer to completely different financial instruments such as government bonds or, less commonly, to all kinds of marketable securities.

a. Share
b. Margin
c. Procter ' Gamble
d. Bucket shop

30. _________ is that which is owed; usually referencing assets owed, but the term can cover other obligations. In the case of assets, _________ is a means of using future purchasing power in the present before a summation has been earned. Some companies and corporations use _________ as a part of their overall corporate finance strategy.

a. Partial Payment
b. Cross-collateralization
c. Credit cycle
d. Debt

31. In finance and economics, _________ or divestiture is the reduction of some kind of asset for either financial goals or ethical objectives. A _________ is the opposite of an investment.

Often the term is used as a means to grow financially in which a company sells off a business unit in order to focus their resources on a market it judges to be more profitable, or promising.

a. Late trading
b. Portfolio investment
c. Divestment
d. Certificate in Investment Performance Measurement

32. A _________ is a new organization or entity formed by a split from a larger one, such as a television series based on a pre-existing one, or a new company formed from a university research group or business incubator. In literature, especially in milieu-based popular fictional book series like mysteries, westerns, fantasy, or science fiction, the term sub-series is generally used instead of _________, but with essentially the same meaning.

_________s as a descriptive term can also include a dissenting faction of a membership organization, a sect of a cult, or a denomination of a church.

a. 7-Eleven
b. Spin-off
c. 529 plan
d. 4-4-5 Calendar

33. _________ means the inability to pay one's debts as they fall due. Usually used in Business terms, _________ refers to the inability for a 'limited liability' company to pay off debts.

This is defined in two different ways:

Cash flow _________ -

Unable to pay debts as they fall due.

Balance sheet _________ -

Having negative net assets: liabilities exceed assets; or net liabilities.

a. Interest
b. Insolvency
c. AAB
d. A Random Walk Down Wall Street

34. In law, _________ refers to the process by which a company (or part of a company) is brought to an end, and the assets and property of the company redistributed. _________ can also be referred to as winding-up or dissolution, although dissolution technically refers to the last stage of _________. The process of _________ also arises when customs, an authority or agency in a country responsible for collecting and safeguarding customs duties, determines the final computation or ascertainment of the duties or drawback accruing on an entry.

a. Debt settlement
b. 529 plan
c. 4-4-5 Calendar
d. Liquidation

35. _________ is a legally declared inability or impairment of ability of an individual or organization to pay their creditors. Creditors may file a _________ petition against a debtor ('involuntary _________') in an effort to recoup a portion of what they are owed or initiate a restructuring. In the majority of cases, however, _________ is initiated by the debtor (a 'voluntary _________' that is filed by the bankrupt individual or organization.)

a. Bankruptcy
b. Debt settlement
c. 529 plan
d. 4-4-5 Calendar

36. A _________ is a party (e.g. person, organization, company, or government) that has a claim to the services of a second party. The first party, in general, has provided some property or service to the second party under the assumption (usually enforced by contract) that the second party will return an equivalent property or service. The second party is frequently called a debtor or borrower.

a. False billing
b. NOPLAT
c. Redemption value
d. Creditor

37. _________ is a process by which a firm can obtain the use of a certain fixed assets for which it must pay a series of contractual, periodic, tax deductable payments. The lessee is the receiver of the services or the assets under the lease contract and the lessor is the owner of the assets. The relationship between the tenant and the landlord is called a tenancy, and can be for a fixed or an indefinite period of time (called the term of the lease).

a. Foreign Corrupt Practices Act
b. Quiet period
c. Leasing
d. Royalties

38. A _________ is a pool of assets forming an independent legal entity that are bought with the contributions to a pension plan for the exclusive purpose of financing pension plan benefits.

_________s are important shareholders of listed and private companies. They are especially important to the stock market where large institutional investors like the Ontario Teachers' Pension Plan dominate.

a. Leverage
b. Limited liability company
c. Leveraged buyout
d. Pension fund

39. The institution most often referenced by the word '_________' is a public or publicly traded _________, the shares of which are traded on a public stock exchange (e.g., the New York Stock Exchange or Nasdaq in the United States) where shares of stock of _________s are bought and sold by and to the general public. Most of the largest businesses in the world are publicly traded _________s. However, the majority of _________s are said to be closely held, privately held or close _________s, meaning that no ready market exists for the trading of shares.

a. Protect
b. Depository Trust Company
c. Federal Home Loan Mortgage Corporation
d. Corporation

40. _________ is a process that allows a private or public company - or a sovereign entity - facing cash flow problems and financial distress, to reduce and renegotiate its delinquent debts in order to improve or restore liquidity and rehabilitate so that it can continue its operations.

Out-of court restructurings, also known as workouts, are increasingly becoming a global reality. A _________ is usually less expensive and a preferable alternative to bankruptcy.

a. Prepayment
b. Commuted cash value
c. Debt restructuring
d. Cost of living

1. The institution most often referenced by the word '_________' is a public or publicly traded _________, the shares of which are traded on a public stock exchange (e.g., the New York Stock Exchange or Nasdaq in the United States) where shares of stock of _________s are bought and sold by and to the general public. Most of the largest businesses in the world are publicly traded _________s. However, the majority of _________s are said to be closely held, privately held or close _________s, meaning that no ready market exists for the trading of shares.

a. Federal Home Loan Mortgage Corporation
b. Protect
c. Corporation
d. Depository Trust Company

2. _________ in its classic form is defined as a company from one country making a physical investment into building a factory in another country. It is the establishment of an enterprise by a foreigner. Its definition can be extended to include investments made to acquire lasting interest in enterprises operating outside of the economy of the investor.

a. MicroPlace
b. Dow Jones ' Company
c. Public company
d. Foreign direct investment

3. _________ is the branch of economics that studies the dynamics of exchange rates, foreign investment, and how these affect international trade. It also studies international projects, international investments and capital flows, and trade deficits. It includes the study of futures, options and currency swaps.

a. AAB
b. A Random Walk Down Wall Street
c. ABN Amro
d. International finance

4. In economics and finance, _________ represents passive holdings of securities such as foreign stocks, bonds, or other financial assets, none of which entails active management or control of the securities' issuer by the investor; where such control exists, it is known as foreign direct investment. Generally, this means the investor holds less than 10% of the total shares or less than the amount needed to hold the majority vote.

Some examples of _________ are:

- purchase of shares in a foreign company.
- purchase of bonds issued by a foreign government.
- acquisition of assets in a foreign country.

Factors affecting international _________:

- tax rates on interest or dividends (investors will normally prefer countries where the tax rates are relatively low)
- interest rates (money tends to flow to countries with high interest rates)
- exchange rates (foreign investors may be attracted if the local currency is expected to strengthen)

_________ is part of the capital account on the balance of payments statistics.

a. Tactical asset allocation
b. Portable alpha
c. Divestment
d. Portfolio investment

5. In finance, the _________ between two currencies specifies how much one currency is worth in terms of the other. For example an _________ of 102 Japanese yen to the United States dollar means that JPY 102 is worth the same as USD 1. The foreign exchange market is one of the largest markets in the world.

a. ABN Amro
b. Exchange rate
c. A Random Walk Down Wall Street
d. AAB

6. The _________ is where currency trading takes place. It is where banks and other official institutions facilitate the buying and selling of foreign currencies. FX transactions typically involve one party purchasing a quantity of one currency in exchange for paying a quantity of another.

a. Foreign exchange option
b. Floating exchange rate
c. Spot market
d. Foreign exchange market

7. _________ are a currency pair that does not include USD, such as GBP/JPY. Pairs that involve the EUR are called euro crosses, such as EUR/GBP. All other currency pairs (those that don't involve USD or EUR) are generally referred to as _________.

a. 529 plan
b. Cross rates
c. 4-4-5 Calendar
d. Foreign exchange risk

8. _________ is a form of risk that arises from the change in price of one currency against another. Whenever investors or companies have assets or business operations across national borders, they face _________ if their positions are not hedged.

- Transaction risk is the risk that exchange rates will change unfavourably over time. It can be hedged against using forward currency contracts;
- Translation risk is an accounting risk, proportional to the amount of assets held in foreign currencies. Changes in the exchange rate over time will render a report inaccurate, and so assets are usually balanced by borrowings in that currency.

The exchange risk associated with a foreign denominated instrument is a key element in foreign investment. This risk flows from differential monetary policy and growth in real productivity, which results in differential inflation rates.

a. Credit risk
b. Market risk
c. Tracking error
d. Currency risk

9. The _________ or forward rate is the agreed upon price of an asset in a forward contract. Using the rational pricing assumption, we can express the _________ in terms of the spot price and any dividends etc., so that there is no possibility for arbitrage.

The _________ is given by:

where

F is the _________ to be paid at time T
e^x is the exponential function
r is the risk-free interest rate
q is the cost-of-carry
S_0 is the spot price of the asset (i.e. what it would sell for at time 0)
D_i is a dividend which is guaranteed to be paid at time t_i where $0 < t_i < T$.

The two questions here are what price the short position (the seller of the asset) should offer to maximize his gain, and what price the long position (the buyer of the asset) should accept to maximize his gain?

At the very least we know that both do not want to lose any money in the deal.

a. Financial Gerontology
b. Security interest
c. Biweekly Mortgage
d. Forward price

10. The _________ of a commodity, a security or a currency is the price that is quoted for immediate (spot) settlement (payment and delivery.) Spot settlement is normally one or two business days from trade date. This is in contrast with the forward price established in a forward contract or futures contract, where contract terms (price) are set now, but delivery and payment will occur at a future date.

a. Market anomaly
b. Limits to arbitrage
c. Spot rate
d. Long position

11. _________ is an economic model based on price, utility and quantity in a market. It predicts that in a competitive market, price will function to equalize the quantity demanded by consumers, and the quantity supplied by producers, resulting in an economic equilibrium of price and quantity. Similarly, an increase in the number of workers tends to result in lower wages and vice-versa.

a. Price channel
b. Rural credit cooperatives
c. Loan participation
d. Supply and demand

12. _________ (in a financial context) is the assumption of the risk of loss, in return for the uncertain possibility of a reward. Only if one may safely say that a particular position involves no risk may one say, strictly speaking, that such a position represents an 'investment.' Financial _________ involves the buying, holding, selling, and short-selling of stocks, bonds, commodities, currencies, collectibles, real estate, derivatives, or any valuable financial instrument to profit from fluctuations in its price as opposed to buying it for use or for income via methods such as dividends or interest. _________ represents one of four market roles in Western financial markets, distinct from hedging, long- or short-term investing, and arbitrage.

a. Central Securities Depository
b. Forward market
c. Market anomaly
d. Speculation

13. The _________ is the difference between a nation's exports of goods and services and its imports of goods and services, if all financial transfers and investments and the like are ignored. A nation is said to have a trade deficit if it is importing more than it exports.

In economics, the current account is one of the two primary components of the balance of payments, the other being the capital account.

a. Value added
b. Supply shock
c. Demand shock
d. Balance of trade

14. _________ is the quality of paper money substitutes which entitles the holder to redeem them on demand into money proper.

Historically, the banknote has followed a common or very similar pattern in the western nations. Originally decentralized and issued from various independent banks, it was gradually brought under state control and became a monopoly privilege of the central banks.

a. Convertibility
b. Devaluation
c. Petrodollar recycling
d. Functional currency

15. The _________ is the market for securities, where companies and governments can raise longterm funds. The _________ includes the stock market and the bond market. Financial regulators, such as the U.S. Securities and Exchange Commission, oversee the _________s in their designated countries to ensure that investors are protected against fraud.

a. Spot rate
b. Forward market
c. Delta neutral
d. Capital market

16. In finance, a _________ is a debt security, in which the authorized issuer owes the holders a debt and, depending on the terms of the _________, is obliged to pay interest (the coupon) and/or to repay the principal at a later date, termed maturity.

Thus a _________ is a loan: the issuer is the borrower, the _________ holder is the lender, and the coupon is the interest. _________s provide the borrower with external funds to finance long-term investments, or, in the case of government _________s, to finance current expenditure.

a. Convertible bond
b. Catastrophe bonds
c. Puttable bond
d. Bond

17. A _________ is an international bond that is denominated in a currency not native to the country where it is issued. It can be categorised according to the currency in which it is issued. London is one of the centers of the _________ market, but _________s may be traded throughout the world - for example in Singapore or Tokyo.

a. Eurobond
b. Economic entity
c. Interest rate option
d. Education production function

18. _________s are deposits denominated in United States dollars at banks outside the United States, and thus are not under the jurisdiction of the Federal Reserve. Consequently, such deposits are subject to much less regulation than similar deposits within the United States, allowing for higher margins. There is nothing 'European' about _________ deposits; a US dollar-denominated deposit in Tokyo or Caracas would likewise be deemed _________ deposits.

a. Eurodollar
b. A Random Walk Down Wall Street
c. ABN Amro
d. AAB

19. The _________ is a financial market where participants buy and sell debt securities, usually in the form of bonds. As of 2006, the size of the international _________ is an estimated $45 trillion, of which the size of the outstanding U.S. _________ debt was $25.2 trillion.

Nearly all of the $923 billion average daily trading volume in the U.S. _________ takes place between broker-dealers and large institutions in a decentralized, over-the-counter market.

a. Fixed income
b. 4-4-5 Calendar
c. 529 plan
d. Bond market

20. _________ is a type of risk faced by investors, corporations, and governments. It is a risk that can be understood and managed with proper aforethought and investment.

Broadly, _________ refers to the complications businesses and governments may face as a result of what are commonly referred to as political decisions--or 'any political change that alters the expected outcome and value of a given economic action by changing the probability of achieving business objectives.' .

a. Single-index model
b. Mid price
c. Capital asset
d. Political risk

21. The _________ of 1977 (15 U.S.C. Â§Â§ 78dd-1, et seq.) is a United States federal law known primarily for two of its main provisions, one that addresses accounting transparency requirements under the Securities Exchange Act of 1934 and another concerning bribery of foreign officials.

a. Fair debt collection
b. Federal Deposit Insurance Corporation Improvement Act
c. Foreign Corrupt Practices Act
d. Competition law

Chapter 1

1. d	2. a	3. d	4. b	5. c	6. d	7. d	8. a	9. d	10. d
11. d	12. d	13. d	14. c	15. a	16. a	17. d	18. d	19. d	20. d
21. c	22. a	23. d	24. d	25. d	26. b	27. d	28. d	29. d	30. a
31. b	32. d								

Chapter 2

1. d	2. d	3. b	4. d	5. b	6. d	7. d	8. d	9. d	10. d
11. b	12. d	13. d	14. d	15. d	16. b	17. a	18. d	19. c	20. d
21. a	22. d	23. d	24. d	25. b	26. d	27. d	28. b	29. b	30. d
31. d	32. d	33. d	34. d	35. d	36. c	37. d	38. d	39. c	40. d
41. a	42. c	43. b	44. d	45. d	46. a	47. b	48. d	49. d	50. b
51. c	52. c	53. d	54. d	55. d	56. d	57. b	58. b	59. d	60. d
61. d	62. a	63. d	64. d	65. a					

Chapter 3

1. a	2. c	3. c	4. d	5. c	6. d	7. b	8. d	9. b	10. d
11. b	12. d	13. b	14. a	15. a	16. c	17. c	18. c	19. c	20. d
21. a	22. d	23. d	24. d	25. c	26. d	27. c	28. a	29. d	30. d
31. a	32. d	33. c	34. d	35. d	36. d	37. a	38. b	39. a	40. c
41. b	42. b	43. b	44. b						

Chapter 4

1. d	2. d	3. d	4. b	5. d	6. b	7. d	8. d	9. d	10. c
11. d	12. a	13. d	14. d	15. b	16. d	17. a	18. d	19. c	20. a
21. c	22. d	23. d	24. d	25. d	26. b	27. d	28. d	29. d	30. c
31. d	32. d	33. b	34. a	35. c	36. d	37. c	38. a	39. d	40. c
41. a	42. d	43. d	44. d	45. a					

Chapter 5

1. d	2. c	3. d	4. d	5. b	6. b	7. d	8. d	9. b	10. a
11. d	12. d	13. c	14. d	15. c	16. d	17. d	18. d	19. a	20. b
21. c	22. d	23. d	24. b	25. d					

Chapter 6

1. c	2. c	3. d	4. d	5. b	6. c	7. a	8. d	9. b	10. d
11. d	12. d	13. d	14. a	15. d	16. d	17. d	18. b	19. b	20. c
21. d	22. d	23. a	24. d	25. a	26. a	27. b	28. d	29. b	30. b
31. c	32. d	33. c	34. d	35. d	36. d	37. d	38. d	39. d	40. c
41. b	42. d	43. d	44. d	45. d	46. a	47. d	48. b	49. d	50. d
51. d	52. a	53. c	54. c	55. c	56. c	57. b	58. c	59. a	60. b
61. b	62. d	63. b							

Chapter 7

1. b	2. d	3. a	4. d	5. d	6. d	7. c	8. d	9. b	10. d
11. b	12. a	13. c	14. b	15. c	16. d	17. a	18. d	19. d	20. d
21. a	22. a	23. c	24. d	25. d	26. d	27. d	28. d	29. b	30. d
31. d	32. b	33. d	34. d	35. b	36. d	37. c	38. d	39. b	40. d
41. d	42. d	43. a	44. a	45. d	46. a	47. d	48. d	49. d	50. c
51. d	52. d								

Chapter 8

1. c	2. d	3. d	4. d	5. a	6. c	7. b	8. b	9. d	10. d
11. b	12. d	13. d	14. d	15. d	16. c	17. d	18. d	19. a	20. a
21. d	22. c	23. d	24. a	25. d	26. a	27. d	28. c	29. d	30. c

Chapter 9

1. d	2. c	3. c	4. b	5. d	6. d	7. a	8. d	9. b	10. d
11. d	12. b	13. c	14. b	15. d	16. d	17. d	18. d	19. b	20. a

Chapter 10

1. d	2. c	3. a	4. d	5. b	6. c	7. b	8. d	9. c	10. a
11. d	12. d	13. d	14. d	15. c	16. b	17. d			

Chapter 11

1. c	2. d	3. a	4. d	5. b	6. d	7. b	8. c	9. a	10. c
11. b	12. c	13. b	14. d	15. d	16. b	17. c	18. d	19. d	20. d
21. b									

Chapter 12

1. d	2. d	3. d	4. d	5. d	6. a	7. b	8. d	9. a	10. d
11. a	12. b	13. c	14. d	15. d	16. d	17. a	18. d	19. a	20. b
21. d	22. d	23. a	24. d	25. a					

Chapter 13

1. d	2. a	3. b	4. d	5. d	6. d	7. d	8. a	9. d	10. d
11. d	12. c	13. d	14. d	15. a	16. a	17. c	18. b	19. c	20. d
21. d	22. a	23. c	24. b	25. b	26. a	27. c	28. d		

Chapter 14

1. a	2. a	3. a	4. b	5. d	6. b	7. a	8. c	9. d	10. d
11. c	12. b	13. c	14. d	15. a	16. a	17. a	18. a	19. d	20. b
21. b	22. d	23. d	24. a						

Chapter 15

1. d	2. a	3. c	4. d	5. b	6. b	7. d	8. b	9. d	10. d
11. d	12. d	13. d	14. d	15. d	16. b	17. d	18. d	19. d	20. a
21. d	22. b	23. d	24. d	25. b	26. b	27. d	28. d	29. d	30. c
31. c	32. a	33. d	34. b	35. d	36. d	37. a	38. d	39. d	40. b
41. d	42. d								

Chapter 16

1. a	2. b	3. d	4. a	5. b	6. c	7. c	8. b	9. b	10. b
11. c	12. d	13. d	14. d	15. d					

Chapter 17

1. c	2. d	3. c	4. d	5. b	6. d	7. a	8. d	9. b	10. d
11. d	12. d	13. a	14. a	15. a	16. c	17. c	18. d	19. b	20. a
21. a	22. d	23. d	24. a	25. c	26. b	27. c	28. d	29. a	30. d
31. c	32. b	33. b	34. d	35. a	36. d	37. c	38. d	39. d	40. c

Chapter 18

1. c	2. d	3. d	4. d	5. b	6. d	7. b	8. d	9. d	10. c
11. d	12. d	13. d	14. a	15. d	16. d	17. a	18. a	19. d	20. d
21. c									

www.ingramcontent.com/pod-product-compliance
Lightning Source LLC
Chambersburg PA
CBHW082042230426
43670CB00016B/2751
* 9 7 8 1 4 2 8 8 6 9 9 9 8 *